C-3393   CAREER EXAMINATION SERIES

*This is your
PASSBOOK for...*

Justice Court Clerk

*Test Preparation Study Guide
Questions & Answers*

COPYRIGHT NOTICE

This book is SOLELY intended for, is sold ONLY to, and its use is RESTRICTED to individual, bona fide applicants or candidates who qualify by virtue of having seriously filed applications for appropriate license, certificate, professional and/or promotional advancement, higher school matriculation, scholarship, or other legitimate requirements of education and/or governmental authorities.

This book is NOT intended for use, class instruction, tutoring, training, duplication, copying, reprinting, excerption, or adaptation, etc., by:

1) Other publishers
2) Proprietors and/or Instructors of "Coaching" and/or Preparatory Courses
3) Personnel and/or Training Divisions of commercial, industrial, and governmental organizations
4) Schools, colleges, or universities and/or their departments and staffs, including teachers and other personnel
5) Testing Agencies or Bureaus
6) Study groups which seek by the purchase of a single volume to copy and/or duplicate and/or adapt this material for use by the group as a whole without having purchased individual volumes for each of the members of the group
7) Et al.

Such persons would be in violation of appropriate Federal and State statutes.

PROVISION OF LICENSING AGREEMENTS – Recognized educational, commercial, industrial, and governmental institutions and organizations, and others legitimately engaged in educational pursuits, including training, testing, and measurement activities, may address request for a licensing agreement to the copyright owners, who will determine whether, and under what conditions, including fees and charges, the materials in this book may be used them. In other words, a licensing facility exists for the legitimate use of the material in this book on other than an individual basis. However, it is asseverated and affirmed here that the material in this book CANNOT be used without the receipt of the express permission of such a licensing agreement from the Publishers. Inquiries re licensing should be addressed to the company, attention rights and permissions department.

All rights reserved, including the right of reproduction in whole or in part, in any form or by any means, electronic or mechanical, including photocopying, recording, or by any information storage and retrieval system, without permission in writing from the Publisher.

Copyright © 2024 by
National Learning Corporation

212 Michael Drive, Syosset, NY 11791
(516) 921-8888 • www.passbooks.com
E-mail: info@passbooks.com

PUBLISHED IN THE UNITED STATES OF AMERICA

PASSBOOK® SERIES

THE *PASSBOOK® SERIES* has been created to prepare applicants and candidates for the ultimate academic battlefield – the examination room.

At some time in our lives, each and every one of us may be required to take an examination – for validation, matriculation, admission, qualification, registration, certification, or licensure.

Based on the assumption that every applicant or candidate has met the basic formal educational standards, has taken the required number of courses, and read the necessary texts, the *PASSBOOK® SERIES* furnishes the one special preparation which may assure passing with confidence, instead of failing with insecurity. Examination questions – together with answers – are furnished as the basic vehicle for study so that the mysteries of the examination and its compounding difficulties may be eliminated or diminished by a sure method.

This book is meant to help you pass your examination provided that you qualify and are serious in your objective.

The entire field is reviewed through the huge store of content information which is succinctly presented through a provocative and challenging approach – the question-and-answer method.

A climate of success is established by furnishing the correct answers at the end of each test.

You soon learn to recognize types of questions, forms of questions, and patterns of questioning. You may even begin to anticipate expected outcomes.

You perceive that many questions are repeated or adapted so that you can gain acute insights, which may enable you to score many sure points.

You learn how to confront new questions, or types of questions, and to attack them confidently and work out the correct answers.

You note objectives and emphases, and recognize pitfalls and dangers, so that you may make positive educational adjustments.

Moreover, you are kept fully informed in relation to new concepts, methods, practices, and directions in the field.

You discover that you are actually taking the examination all the time: you are preparing for the examination by "taking" an examination, not by reading extraneous and/or supererogatory textbooks.

In short, this PASSBOOK®, used directedly, should be an important factor in helping you to pass your test.

JUSTICE COURT CLERK

DUTIES
An employee in this class performs varied clerical work, in and out of court, requiring some knowledge of statutes and laws governing the practices and procedures of Justice Courts. Work involves responsibility for the preparation and issuance of various legal papers and recording legal matters pertaining to the operation of the court. Work involves contact with attorneys and the general public regarding court functions and procedures. All work is performed according to standard procedures prescribed by state law, judicial determination and administrative directives. Supervision may be exercised over clerical personnel. Work is performed under the supervision of a clerical supervisor or a Justice of the Court. Does related work as required.

SCOPE OF THE EXAMINATION
The written test will cover knowledge, skills, and/or abilities in such areas as:
1. Record keeping and organization of data;
2. Clerical operations, including proofreading; and
3. Understanding and interpreting written material, including legal policies and procedures.

HOW TO TAKE A TEST

I. YOU MUST PASS AN EXAMINATION

A. WHAT EVERY CANDIDATE SHOULD KNOW

Examination applicants often ask us for help in preparing for the written test. What can I study in advance? What kinds of questions will be asked? How will the test be given? How will the papers be graded?

As an applicant for a civil service examination, you may be wondering about some of these things. Our purpose here is to suggest effective methods of advance study and to describe civil service examinations.

Your chances for success on this examination can be increased if you know how to prepare. Those "pre-examination jitters" can be reduced if you know what to expect. You can even experience an adventure in good citizenship if you know why civil service exams are given.

B. WHY ARE CIVIL SERVICE EXAMINATIONS GIVEN?

Civil service examinations are important to you in two ways. As a citizen, you want public jobs filled by employees who know how to do their work. As a job seeker, you want a fair chance to compete for that job on an equal footing with other candidates. The best-known means of accomplishing this two-fold goal is the competitive examination.

Exams are widely publicized throughout the nation. They may be administered for jobs in federal, state, city, municipal, town or village governments or agencies.

Any citizen may apply, with some limitations, such as the age or residence of applicants. Your experience and education may be reviewed to see whether you meet the requirements for the particular examination. When these requirements exist, they are reasonable and applied consistently to all applicants. Thus, a competitive examination may cause you some uneasiness now, but it is your privilege and safeguard.

C. HOW ARE CIVIL SERVICE EXAMS DEVELOPED?

Examinations are carefully written by trained technicians who are specialists in the field known as "psychological measurement," in consultation with recognized authorities in the field of work that the test will cover. These experts recommend the subject matter areas or skills to be tested; only those knowledges or skills important to your success on the job are included. The most reliable books and source materials available are used as references. Together, the experts and technicians judge the difficulty level of the questions.

Test technicians know how to phrase questions so that the problem is clearly stated. Their ethics do not permit "trick" or "catch" questions. Questions may have been tried out on sample groups, or subjected to statistical analysis, to determine their usefulness.

Written tests are often used in combination with performance tests, ratings of training and experience, and oral interviews. All of these measures combine to form the best-known means of finding the right person for the right job.

II. HOW TO PASS THE WRITTEN TEST

A. NATURE OF THE EXAMINATION

To prepare intelligently for civil service examinations, you should know how they differ from school examinations you have taken. In school you were assigned certain definite pages to read or subjects to cover. The examination questions were quite detailed and usually emphasized memory. Civil service exams, on the other hand, try to discover your present ability to perform the duties of a position, plus your potentiality to learn these duties. In other words, a civil service exam attempts to predict how successful you will be. Questions cover such a broad area that they cannot be as minute and detailed as school exam questions.

In the public service similar kinds of work, or positions, are grouped together in one "class." This process is known as *position-classification*. All the positions in a class are paid according to the salary range for that class. One class title covers all of these positions, and they are all tested by the same examination.

B. FOUR BASIC STEPS

1) Study the announcement

How, then, can you know what subjects to study? Our best answer is: "Learn as much as possible about the class of positions for which you've applied." The exam will test the knowledge, skills and abilities needed to do the work.

Your most valuable source of information about the position you want is the official exam announcement. This announcement lists the training and experience qualifications. Check these standards and apply only if you come reasonably close to meeting them.

The brief description of the position in the examination announcement offers some clues to the subjects which will be tested. Think about the job itself. Review the duties in your mind. Can you perform them, or are there some in which you are rusty? Fill in the blank spots in your preparation.

Many jurisdictions preview the written test in the exam announcement by including a section called "Knowledge and Abilities Required," "Scope of the Examination," or some similar heading. Here you will find out specifically what fields will be tested.

2) Review your own background

Once you learn in general what the position is all about, and what you need to know to do the work, ask yourself which subjects you already know fairly well and which need improvement. You may wonder whether to concentrate on improving your strong areas or on building some background in your fields of weakness. When the announcement has specified "some knowledge" or "considerable knowledge," or has used adjectives like "beginning principles of..." or "advanced ... methods," you can get a clue as to the number and difficulty of questions to be asked in any given field. More questions, and hence broader coverage, would be included for those subjects which are more important in the work. Now weigh your strengths and weaknesses against the job requirements and prepare accordingly.

3) Determine the level of the position

Another way to tell how intensively you should prepare is to understand the level of the job for which you are applying. Is it the entering level? In other words, is this the position in which beginners in a field of work are hired? Or is it an intermediate or advanced level? Sometimes this is indicated by such words as "Junior" or "Senior" in the class title. Other jurisdictions use Roman numerals to designate the level – Clerk I, Clerk II, for example. The word "Supervisor" sometimes appears in the title. If the level is not indicated by the title, check the description of duties. Will you be working under very close supervision, or will you have responsibility for independent decisions in this work?

4) Choose appropriate study materials

Now that you know the subjects to be examined and the relative amount of each subject to be covered, you can choose suitable study materials. For beginning level jobs, or even advanced ones, if you have a pronounced weakness in some aspect of your training, read a modern, standard textbook in that field. Be sure it is up to date and has general coverage. Such books are normally available at your library, and the librarian will be glad to help you locate one. For entry-level positions, questions of appropriate difficulty are chosen -- neither highly advanced questions, nor those too simple. Such questions require careful thought but not advanced training.

If the position for which you are applying is technical or advanced, you will read more advanced, specialized material. If you are already familiar with the basic principles of your field, elementary textbooks would waste your time. Concentrate on advanced textbooks and technical periodicals. Think through the concepts and review difficult problems in your field.

These are all general sources. You can get more ideas on your own initiative, following these leads. For example, training manuals and publications of the government agency which employs workers in your field can be useful, particularly for technical and professional positions. A letter or visit to the government department involved may result in more specific study suggestions, and certainly will provide you with a more definite idea of the exact nature of the position you are seeking.

III. KINDS OF TESTS

Tests are used for purposes other than measuring knowledge and ability to perform specified duties. For some positions, it is equally important to test ability to make adjustments to new situations or to profit from training. In others, basic mental abilities not dependent on information are essential. Questions which test these things may not appear as pertinent to the duties of the position as those which test for knowledge and information. Yet they are often highly important parts of a fair examination. For very general questions, it is almost impossible to help you direct your study efforts. What we can do is to point out some of the more common of these general abilities needed in public service positions and describe some typical questions.

1) General information

Broad, general information has been found useful for predicting job success in some kinds of work. This is tested in a variety of ways, from vocabulary lists to questions about current events. Basic background in some field of work, such as sociology or economics, may be sampled in a group of questions. Often these are principles which have become familiar to most persons through exposure rather than through formal training. It is difficult to advise you how to study for these questions; being alert to the world around you is our best suggestion.

2) Verbal ability

An example of an ability needed in many positions is verbal or language ability. Verbal ability is, in brief, the ability to use and understand words. Vocabulary and grammar tests are typical measures of this ability. Reading comprehension or paragraph interpretation questions are common in many kinds of civil service tests. You are given a paragraph of written material and asked to find its central meaning.

3) Numerical ability

Number skills can be tested by the familiar arithmetic problem, by checking paired lists of numbers to see which are alike and which are different, or by interpreting charts and graphs. In the latter test, a graph may be printed in the test booklet which you are asked to use as the basis for answering questions.

4) Observation

A popular test for law-enforcement positions is the observation test. A picture is shown to you for several minutes, then taken away. Questions about the picture test your ability to observe both details and larger elements.

5) Following directions

In many positions in the public service, the employee must be able to carry out written instructions dependably and accurately. You may be given a chart with several columns, each column listing a variety of information. The questions require you to carry out directions involving the information given in the chart.

6) Skills and aptitudes

Performance tests effectively measure some manual skills and aptitudes. When the skill is one in which you are trained, such as typing or shorthand, you can practice. These tests are often very much like those given in business school or high school courses. For many of the other skills and aptitudes, however, no short-time preparation can be made. Skills and abilities natural to you or that you have developed throughout your lifetime are being tested.

Many of the general questions just described provide all the data needed to answer the questions and ask you to use your reasoning ability to find the answers. Your best preparation for these tests, as well as for tests of facts and ideas, is to be at your physical and mental best. You, no doubt, have your own methods of getting into an exam-taking mood and keeping "in shape." The next section lists some ideas on this subject.

IV. KINDS OF QUESTIONS

Only rarely is the "essay" question, which you answer in narrative form, used in civil service tests. Civil service tests are usually of the short-answer type. Full instructions for answering these questions will be given to you at the examination. But in case this is your first experience with short-answer questions and separate answer sheets, here is what you need to know:

1) Multiple-choice Questions

Most popular of the short-answer questions is the "multiple choice" or "best answer" question. It can be used, for example, to test for factual knowledge, ability to solve problems or judgment in meeting situations found at work.

A multiple-choice question is normally one of three types—
- It can begin with an incomplete statement followed by several possible endings. You are to find the one ending which *best* completes the statement, although some of the others may not be entirely wrong.
- It can also be a complete statement in the form of a question which is answered by choosing one of the statements listed.

- It can be in the form of a problem – again you select the best answer.

Here is an example of a multiple-choice question with a discussion which should give you some clues as to the method for choosing the right answer:

When an employee has a complaint about his assignment, the action which will *best* help him overcome his difficulty is to
    A. discuss his difficulty with his coworkers
    B. take the problem to the head of the organization
    C. take the problem to the person who gave him the assignment
    D. say nothing to anyone about his complaint

In answering this question, you should study each of the choices to find which is best. Consider choice "A" – Certainly an employee may discuss his complaint with fellow employees, but no change or improvement can result, and the complaint remains unresolved. Choice "B" is a poor choice since the head of the organization probably does not know what assignment you have been given, and taking your problem to him is known as "going over the head" of the supervisor. The supervisor, or person who made the assignment, is the person who can clarify it or correct any injustice. Choice "C" is, therefore, correct. To say nothing, as in choice "D," is unwise. Supervisors have and interest in knowing the problems employees are facing, and the employee is seeking a solution to his problem.

2) True/False Questions

The "true/false" or "right/wrong" form of question is sometimes used. Here a complete statement is given. Your job is to decide whether the statement is right or wrong.

SAMPLE: A roaming cell-phone call to a nearby city costs less than a non-roaming call to a distant city.

This statement is wrong, or false, since roaming calls are more expensive.

This is not a complete list of all possible question forms, although most of the others are variations of these common types. You will always get complete directions for answering questions. Be sure you understand *how* to mark your answers – ask questions until you do.

V. RECORDING YOUR ANSWERS

Computer terminals are used more and more today for many different kinds of exams.
For an examination with very few applicants, you may be told to record your answers in the test booklet itself. Separate answer sheets are much more common. If this separate answer sheet is to be scored by machine – and this is often the case – it is highly important that you mark your answers correctly in order to get credit.
An electronic scoring machine is often used in civil service offices because of the speed with which papers can be scored. Machine-scored answer sheets must be marked with a pencil, which will be given to you. This pencil has a high graphite content which responds to the electronic scoring machine. As a matter of fact, stray dots may register as answers, so do not let your pencil rest on the answer sheet while you are pondering the correct answer. Also, if your pencil lead breaks or is otherwise defective, ask for another.

Since the answer sheet will be dropped in a slot in the scoring machine, be careful not to bend the corners or get the paper crumpled.

The answer sheet normally has five vertical columns of numbers, with 30 numbers to a column. These numbers correspond to the question numbers in your test booklet. After each number, going across the page are four or five pairs of dotted lines. These short dotted lines have small letters or numbers above them. The first two pairs may also have a "T" or "F" above the letters. This indicates that the first two pairs only are to be used if the questions are of the true-false type. If the questions are multiple choice, disregard the "T" and "F" and pay attention only to the small letters or numbers.

Answer your questions in the manner of the sample that follows:

32. The largest city in the United States is
    A. Washington, D.C.
    B. New York City
    C. Chicago
    D. Detroit
    E. San Francisco

1) Choose the answer you think is best. (New York City is the largest, so "B" is correct.)
2) Find the row of dotted lines numbered the same as the question you are answering. (Find row number 32)
3) Find the pair of dotted lines corresponding to the answer. (Find the pair of lines under the mark "B.")
4) Make a solid black mark between the dotted lines.

VI. BEFORE THE TEST

Common sense will help you find procedures to follow to get ready for an examination. Too many of us, however, overlook these sensible measures. Indeed, nervousness and fatigue have been found to be the most serious reasons why applicants fail to do their best on civil service tests. Here is a list of reminders:

- Begin your preparation early – Don't wait until the last minute to go scurrying around for books and materials or to find out what the position is all about.
- Prepare continuously – An hour a night for a week is better than an all-night cram session. This has been definitely established. What is more, a night a week for a month will return better dividends than crowding your study into a shorter period of time.
- Locate the place of the exam – You have been sent a notice telling you when and where to report for the examination. If the location is in a different town or otherwise unfamiliar to you, it would be well to inquire the best route and learn something about the building.
- Relax the night before the test – Allow your mind to rest. Do not study at all that night. Plan some mild recreation or diversion; then go to bed early and get a good night's sleep.
- Get up early enough to make a leisurely trip to the place for the test – This way unforeseen events, traffic snarls, unfamiliar buildings, etc. will not upset you.
- Dress comfortably – A written test is not a fashion show. You will be known by number and not by name, so wear something comfortable.

- Leave excess paraphernalia at home – Shopping bags and odd bundles will get in your way. You need bring only the items mentioned in the official notice you received; usually everything you need is provided. Do not bring reference books to the exam. They will only confuse those last minutes and be taken away from you when in the test room.
- Arrive somewhat ahead of time – If because of transportation schedules you must get there very early, bring a newspaper or magazine to take your mind off yourself while waiting.
- Locate the examination room – When you have found the proper room, you will be directed to the seat or part of the room where you will sit. Sometimes you are given a sheet of instructions to read while you are waiting. Do not fill out any forms until you are told to do so; just read them and be prepared.
- Relax and prepare to listen to the instructions
- If you have any physical problem that may keep you from doing your best, be sure to tell the test administrator. If you are sick or in poor health, you really cannot do your best on the exam. You can come back and take the test some other time.

VII. AT THE TEST

The day of the test is here and you have the test booklet in your hand. The temptation to get going is very strong. Caution! There is more to success than knowing the right answers. You must know how to identify your papers and understand variations in the type of short-answer question used in this particular examination. Follow these suggestions for maximum results from your efforts:

1) Cooperate with the monitor

The test administrator has a duty to create a situation in which you can be as much at ease as possible. He will give instructions, tell you when to begin, check to see that you are marking your answer sheet correctly, and so on. He is not there to guard you, although he will see that your competitors do not take unfair advantage. He wants to help you do your best.

2) Listen to all instructions

Don't jump the gun! Wait until you understand all directions. In most civil service tests you get more time than you need to answer the questions. So don't be in a hurry. Read each word of instructions until you clearly understand the meaning. Study the examples, listen to all announcements and follow directions. Ask questions if you do not understand what to do.

3) Identify your papers

Civil service exams are usually identified by number only. You will be assigned a number; you must not put your name on your test papers. Be sure to copy your number correctly. Since more than one exam may be given, copy your exact examination title.

4) Plan your time

Unless you are told that a test is a "speed" or "rate of work" test, speed itself is usually not important. Time enough to answer all the questions will be provided, but this does not mean that you have all day. An overall time limit has been set. Divide the total time (in minutes) by the number of questions to determine the approximate time you have for each question.

5) Do not linger over difficult questions

If you come across a difficult question, mark it with a paper clip (useful to have along) and come back to it when you have been through the booklet. One caution if you do this – be sure to skip a number on your answer sheet as well. Check often to be sure that you have not lost your place and that you are marking in the row numbered the same as the question you are answering.

6) Read the questions

Be sure you know what the question asks! Many capable people are unsuccessful because they failed to *read* the questions correctly.

7) Answer all questions

Unless you have been instructed that a penalty will be deducted for incorrect answers, it is better to guess than to omit a question.

8) Speed tests

It is often better NOT to guess on speed tests. It has been found that on timed tests people are tempted to spend the last few seconds before time is called in marking answers at random – without even reading them – in the hope of picking up a few extra points. To discourage this practice, the instructions may warn you that your score will be "corrected" for guessing. That is, a penalty will be applied. The incorrect answers will be deducted from the correct ones, or some other penalty formula will be used.

9) Review your answers

If you finish before time is called, go back to the questions you guessed or omitted to give them further thought. Review other answers if you have time.

10) Return your test materials

If you are ready to leave before others have finished or time is called, take ALL your materials to the monitor and leave quietly. Never take any test material with you. The monitor can discover whose papers are not complete, and taking a test booklet may be grounds for disqualification.

VIII. EXAMINATION TECHNIQUES

1) Read the general instructions carefully. These are usually printed on the first page of the exam booklet. As a rule, these instructions refer to the timing of the examination; the fact that you should not start work until the signal and must stop work at a signal, etc. If there are any *special* instructions, such as a choice of questions to be answered, make sure that you note this instruction carefully.

2) When you are ready to start work on the examination, that is as soon as the signal has been given, read the instructions to each question booklet, underline any key words or phrases, such as *least, best, outline, describe* and the like. In this way you will tend to answer as requested rather than discover on reviewing your paper that you *listed without describing*, that you selected the *worst* choice rather than the *best* choice, etc.

3) If the examination is of the objective or multiple-choice type – that is, each question will also give a series of possible answers: A, B, C or D, and you are called upon to select the best answer and write the letter next to that answer on your answer paper – it is advisable to start answering each question in turn. There may be anywhere from 50 to 100 such questions in the three or four hours allotted and you can see how much time would be taken if you read through all the questions before beginning to answer any. Furthermore, if you come across a question or group of questions which you know would be difficult to answer, it would undoubtedly affect your handling of all the other questions.

4) If the examination is of the essay type and contains but a few questions, it is a moot point as to whether you should read all the questions before starting to answer any one. Of course, if you are given a choice – say five out of seven and the like – then it is essential to read all the questions so you can eliminate the two that are most difficult. If, however, you are asked to answer all the questions, there may be danger in trying to answer the easiest one first because you may find that you will spend too much time on it. The best technique is to answer the first question, then proceed to the second, etc.

5) Time your answers. Before the exam begins, write down the time it started, then add the time allowed for the examination and write down the time it must be completed, then divide the time available somewhat as follows:
   - If 3-1/2 hours are allowed, that would be 210 minutes. If you have 80 objective-type questions, that would be an average of 2-1/2 minutes per question. Allow yourself no more than 2 minutes per question, or a total of 160 minutes, which will permit about 50 minutes to review.
   - If for the time allotment of 210 minutes there are 7 essay questions to answer, that would average about 30 minutes a question. Give yourself only 25 minutes per question so that you have about 35 minutes to review.

6) The most important instruction is to *read each question* and make sure you know what is wanted. The second most important instruction is to *time yourself properly* so that you answer every question. The third most important instruction is to *answer every question*. Guess if you have to but include something for each question. Remember that you will receive no credit for a blank and will probably receive some credit if you write something in answer to an essay question. If you guess a letter – say "B" for a multiple-choice question – you may have guessed right. If you leave a blank as an answer to a multiple-choice question, the examiners may respect your feelings but it will not add a point to your score. Some exams may penalize you for wrong answers, so in such cases *only*, you may not want to guess unless you have some basis for your answer.

7) Suggestions
   a. Objective-type questions
      1. Examine the question booklet for proper sequence of pages and questions
      2. Read all instructions carefully
      3. Skip any question which seems too difficult; return to it after all other questions have been answered
      4. Apportion your time properly; do not spend too much time on any single question or group of questions

5. Note and underline key words – *all, most, fewest, least, best, worst, same, opposite,* etc.
6. Pay particular attention to negatives
7. Note unusual option, e.g., unduly long, short, complex, different or similar in content to the body of the question
8. Observe the use of "hedging" words – *probably, may, most likely,* etc.
9. Make sure that your answer is put next to the same number as the question
10. Do not second-guess unless you have good reason to believe the second answer is definitely more correct
11. Cross out original answer if you decide another answer is more accurate; do not erase until you are ready to hand your paper in
12. Answer all questions; guess unless instructed otherwise
13. Leave time for review

b. Essay questions
1. Read each question carefully
2. Determine exactly what is wanted. Underline key words or phrases.
3. Decide on outline or paragraph answer
4. Include many different points and elements unless asked to develop any one or two points or elements
5. Show impartiality by giving pros and cons unless directed to select one side only
6. Make and write down any assumptions you find necessary to answer the questions
7. Watch your English, grammar, punctuation and choice of words
8. Time your answers; don't crowd material

8) Answering the essay question

Most essay questions can be answered by framing the specific response around several key words or ideas. Here are a few such key words or ideas:

M's: manpower, materials, methods, money, management
P's: purpose, program, policy, plan, procedure, practice, problems, pitfalls, personnel, public relations

a. Six basic steps in handling problems:
1. Preliminary plan and background development
2. Collect information, data and facts
3. Analyze and interpret information, data and facts
4. Analyze and develop solutions as well as make recommendations
5. Prepare report and sell recommendations
6. Install recommendations and follow up effectiveness

b. Pitfalls to avoid
1. *Taking things for granted* – A statement of the situation does not necessarily imply that each of the elements is necessarily true; for example, a complaint may be invalid and biased so that all that can be taken for granted is that a complaint has been registered

2. *Considering only one side of a situation* – Wherever possible, indicate several alternatives and then point out the reasons you selected the best one
3. *Failing to indicate follow up* – Whenever your answer indicates action on your part, make certain that you will take proper follow-up action to see how successful your recommendations, procedures or actions turn out to be
4. *Taking too long in answering any single question* – Remember to time your answers properly

IX. AFTER THE TEST

Scoring procedures differ in detail among civil service jurisdictions although the general principles are the same. Whether the papers are hand-scored or graded by machine we have described, they are nearly always graded by number. That is, the person who marks the paper knows only the number – never the name – of the applicant. Not until all the papers have been graded will they be matched with names. If other tests, such as training and experience or oral interview ratings have been given, scores will be combined. Different parts of the examination usually have different weights. For example, the written test might count 60 percent of the final grade, and a rating of training and experience 40 percent. In many jurisdictions, veterans will have a certain number of points added to their grades.

After the final grade has been determined, the names are placed in grade order and an eligible list is established. There are various methods for resolving ties between those who get the same final grade – probably the most common is to place first the name of the person whose application was received first. Job offers are made from the eligible list in the order the names appear on it. You will be notified of your grade and your rank as soon as all these computations have been made. This will be done as rapidly as possible.

People who are found to meet the requirements in the announcement are called "eligibles." Their names are put on a list of eligible candidates. An eligible's chances of getting a job depend on how high he stands on this list and how fast agencies are filling jobs from the list.

When a job is to be filled from a list of eligibles, the agency asks for the names of people on the list of eligibles for that job. When the civil service commission receives this request, it sends to the agency the names of the three people highest on this list. Or, if the job to be filled has specialized requirements, the office sends the agency the names of the top three persons who meet these requirements from the general list.

The appointing officer makes a choice from among the three people whose names were sent to him. If the selected person accepts the appointment, the names of the others are put back on the list to be considered for future openings.

That is the rule in hiring from all kinds of eligible lists, whether they are for typist, carpenter, chemist, or something else. For every vacancy, the appointing officer has his choice of any one of the top three eligibles on the list. This explains why the person whose name is on top of the list sometimes does not get an appointment when some of the persons lower on the list do. If the appointing officer chooses the second or third eligible, the No. 1 eligible does not get a job at once, but stays on the list until he is appointed or the list is terminated.

X. HOW TO PASS THE INTERVIEW TEST

The examination for which you applied requires an oral interview test. You have already taken the written test and you are now being called for the interview test – the final part of the formal examination.

You may think that it is not possible to prepare for an interview test and that there are no procedures to follow during an interview. Our purpose is to point out some things you can do in advance that will help you and some good rules to follow and pitfalls to avoid while you are being interviewed.

What is an interview supposed to test?

The written examination is designed to test the technical knowledge and competence of the candidate; the oral is designed to evaluate intangible qualities, not readily measured otherwise, and to establish a list showing the relative fitness of each candidate – as measured against his competitors – for the position sought. Scoring is not on the basis of "right" and "wrong," but on a sliding scale of values ranging from "not passable" to "outstanding." As a matter of fact, it is possible to achieve a relatively low score without a single "incorrect" answer because of evident weakness in the qualities being measured.

Occasionally, an examination may consist entirely of an oral test – either an individual or a group oral. In such cases, information is sought concerning the technical knowledges and abilities of the candidate, since there has been no written examination for this purpose. More commonly, however, an oral test is used to supplement a written examination.

Who conducts interviews?

The composition of oral boards varies among different jurisdictions. In nearly all, a representative of the personnel department serves as chairman. One of the members of the board may be a representative of the department in which the candidate would work. In some cases, "outside experts" are used, and, frequently, a businessman or some other representative of the general public is asked to serve. Labor and management or other special groups may be represented. The aim is to secure the services of experts in the appropriate field.

However the board is composed, it is a good idea (and not at all improper or unethical) to ascertain in advance of the interview who the members are and what groups they represent. When you are introduced to them, you will have some idea of their backgrounds and interests, and at least you will not stutter and stammer over their names.

What should be done before the interview?

While knowledge about the board members is useful and takes some of the surprise element out of the interview, there is other preparation which is more substantive. It *is* possible to prepare for an oral interview – in several ways:

1) Keep a copy of your application and review it carefully before the interview

This may be the only document before the oral board, and the starting point of the interview. Know what education and experience you have listed there, and the sequence and dates of all of it. Sometimes the board will ask you to review the highlights of your experience for them; you should not have to hem and haw doing it.

2) Study the class specification and the examination announcement

Usually, the oral board has one or both of these to guide them. The qualities, characteristics or knowledges required by the position sought are stated in these documents. They offer valuable clues as to the nature of the oral interview. For example, if the job involves supervisory responsibilities, the announcement will usually indicate that knowledge of modern supervisory methods and the qualifications of the candidate as a supervisor will be tested. If so, you can expect such questions, frequently in the form of a hypothetical situation which you are expected to solve. NEVER go into an oral without knowledge of the duties and responsibilities of the job you seek.

3) Think through each qualification required

Try to visualize the kind of questions you would ask if you were a board member. How well could you answer them? Try especially to appraise your own knowledge and background in each area, *measured against the job sought*, and identify any areas in which you are weak. Be critical and realistic – do not flatter yourself.

4) Do some general reading in areas in which you feel you may be weak

For example, if the job involves supervision and your past experience has NOT, some general reading in supervisory methods and practices, particularly in the field of human relations, might be useful. Do NOT study agency procedures or detailed manuals. The oral board will be testing your understanding and capacity, not your memory.

5) Get a good night's sleep and watch your general health and mental attitude

You will want a clear head at the interview. Take care of a cold or any other minor ailment, and of course, no hangovers.

What should be done on the day of the interview?

Now comes the day of the interview itself. Give yourself plenty of time to get there. Plan to arrive somewhat ahead of the scheduled time, particularly if your appointment is in the fore part of the day. If a previous candidate fails to appear, the board might be ready for you a bit early. By early afternoon an oral board is almost invariably behind schedule if there are many candidates, and you may have to wait. Take along a book or magazine to read, or your application to review, but leave any extraneous material in the waiting room when you go in for your interview. In any event, relax and compose yourself.

The matter of dress is important. The board is forming impressions about you – from your experience, your manners, your attitude, and your appearance. Give your personal appearance careful attention. Dress your best, but not your flashiest. Choose conservative, appropriate clothing, and be sure it is immaculate. This is a business interview, and your appearance should indicate that you regard it as such. Besides, being well groomed and properly dressed will help boost your confidence.

Sooner or later, someone will call your name and escort you into the interview room. *This is it*. From here on you are on your own. It is too late for any more preparation. But remember, you asked for this opportunity to prove your fitness, and you are here because your request was granted.

What happens when you go in?

The usual sequence of events will be as follows: The clerk (who is often the board stenographer) will introduce you to the chairman of the oral board, who will introduce you to the other members of the board. Acknowledge the introductions before you sit down. Do not be surprised if you find a microphone facing you or a stenotypist sitting by. Oral interviews are usually recorded in the event of an appeal or other review.

Usually the chairman of the board will open the interview by reviewing the highlights of your education and work experience from your application – primarily for the benefit of the other members of the board, as well as to get the material into the record. Do not interrupt or comment unless there is an error or significant misinterpretation; if that is the case, do not hesitate. But do not quibble about insignificant matters. Also, he will usually ask you some question about your education, experience or your present job – partly to get you to start talking and to establish the interviewing "rapport." He may start the actual questioning, or turn it over to one of the other members. Frequently, each member undertakes the questioning on a particular area, one in which he is perhaps most competent, so you can expect each member to participate in the examination. Because time is limited, you may also expect some rather abrupt switches in the direction the questioning takes, so do not be upset by it. Normally, a board member will not pursue a single line of questioning unless he discovers a particular strength or weakness.

After each member has participated, the chairman will usually ask whether any member has any further questions, then will ask you if you have anything you wish to add. Unless you are expecting this question, it may floor you. Worse, it may start you off on an extended, extemporaneous speech. The board is not usually seeking more information. The question is principally to offer you a last opportunity to present further qualifications or to indicate that you have nothing to add. So, if you feel that a significant qualification or characteristic has been overlooked, it is proper to point it out in a sentence or so. Do not compliment the board on the thoroughness of their examination – they have been sketchy, and you know it. If you wish, merely say, "No thank you, I have nothing further to add." This is a point where you can "talk yourself out" of a good impression or fail to present an important bit of information. Remember, *you close the interview yourself*.

The chairman will then say, "That is all, Mr. _____, thank you." Do not be startled; the interview is over, and quicker than you think. Thank him, gather your belongings and take your leave. Save your sigh of relief for the other side of the door.

How to put your best foot forward

Throughout this entire process, you may feel that the board individually and collectively is trying to pierce your defenses, seek out your hidden weaknesses and embarrass and confuse you. Actually, this is not true. They are obliged to make an appraisal of your qualifications for the job you are seeking, and they want to see you in your best light. Remember, they must interview all candidates and a non-cooperative candidate may become a failure in spite of their best efforts to bring out his qualifications. Here are 15 suggestions that will help you:

1) Be natural – Keep your attitude confident, not cocky

If you are not confident that you can do the job, do not expect the board to be. Do not apologize for your weaknesses, try to bring out your strong points. The board is interested in a positive, not negative, presentation. Cockiness will antagonize any board member and make him wonder if you are covering up a weakness by a false show of strength.

2) Get comfortable, but don't lounge or sprawl

Sit erectly but not stiffly. A careless posture may lead the board to conclude that you are careless in other things, or at least that you are not impressed by the importance of the occasion. Either conclusion is natural, even if incorrect. Do not fuss with your clothing, a pencil or an ashtray. Your hands may occasionally be useful to emphasize a point; do not let them become a point of distraction.

3) Do not wisecrack or make small talk

This is a serious situation, and your attitude should show that you consider it as such. Further, the time of the board is limited – they do not want to waste it, and neither should you.

4) Do not exaggerate your experience or abilities
In the first place, from information in the application or other interviews and sources, the board may know more about you than you think. Secondly, you probably will not get away with it. An experienced board is rather adept at spotting such a situation, so do not take the chance.

5) If you know a board member, do not make a point of it, yet do not hide it
Certainly you are not fooling him, and probably not the other members of the board. Do not try to take advantage of your acquaintanceship – it will probably do you little good.

6) Do not dominate the interview
Let the board do that. They will give you the clues – do not assume that you have to do all the talking. Realize that the board has a number of questions to ask you, and do not try to take up all the interview time by showing off your extensive knowledge of the answer to the first one.

7) Be attentive
You only have 20 minutes or so, and you should keep your attention at its sharpest throughout. When a member is addressing a problem or question to you, give him your undivided attention. Address your reply principally to him, but do not exclude the other board members.

8) Do not interrupt
A board member may be stating a problem for you to analyze. He will ask you a question when the time comes. Let him state the problem, and wait for the question.

9) Make sure you understand the question
Do not try to answer until you are sure what the question is. If it is not clear, restate it in your own words or ask the board member to clarify it for you. However, do not haggle about minor elements.

10) Reply promptly but not hastily
A common entry on oral board rating sheets is "candidate responded readily," or "candidate hesitated in replies." Respond as promptly and quickly as you can, but do not jump to a hasty, ill-considered answer.

11) Do not be peremptory in your answers
A brief answer is proper – but do not fire your answer back. That is a losing game from your point of view. The board member can probably ask questions much faster than you can answer them.

12) Do not try to create the answer you think the board member wants
He is interested in what kind of mind you have and how it works – not in playing games. Furthermore, he can usually spot this practice and will actually grade you down on it.

13) Do not switch sides in your reply merely to agree with a board member
Frequently, a member will take a contrary position merely to draw you out and to see if you are willing and able to defend your point of view. Do not start a debate, yet do not surrender a good position. If a position is worth taking, it is worth defending.

14) Do not be afraid to admit an error in judgment if you are shown to be wrong

The board knows that you are forced to reply without any opportunity for careful consideration. Your answer may be demonstrably wrong. If so, admit it and get on with the interview.

15) Do not dwell at length on your present job

The opening question may relate to your present assignment. Answer the question but do not go into an extended discussion. You are being examined for a *new* job, not your present one. As a matter of fact, try to phrase ALL your answers in terms of the job for which you are being examined.

Basis of Rating

Probably you will forget most of these "do's" and "don'ts" when you walk into the oral interview room. Even remembering them all will not ensure you a passing grade. Perhaps you did not have the qualifications in the first place. But remembering them will help you to put your best foot forward, without treading on the toes of the board members.

Rumor and popular opinion to the contrary notwithstanding, an oral board wants you to make the best appearance possible. They know you are under pressure – but they also want to see how you respond to it as a guide to what your reaction would be under the pressures of the job you seek. They will be influenced by the degree of poise you display, the personal traits you show and the manner in which you respond.

ABOUT THIS BOOK

This book contains tests divided into Examination Sections. Go through each test, answering every question in the margin. We have also attached a sample answer sheet at the back of the book that can be removed and used. At the end of each test look at the answer key and check your answers. On the ones you got wrong, look at the right answer choice and learn. Do not fill in the answers first. Do not memorize the questions and answers, but understand the answer and principles involved. On your test, the questions will likely be different from the samples. Questions are changed and new ones added. If you understand these past questions you should have success with any changes that arise. Tests may consist of several types of questions. We have additional books on each subject should more study be advisable or necessary for you. Finally, the more you study, the better prepared you will be. This book is intended to be the last thing you study before you walk into the examination room. Prior study of relevant texts is also recommended. NLC publishes some of these in our Fundamental Series. Knowledge and good sense are important factors in passing your exam. Good luck also helps. So now study this Passbook, absorb the material contained within and take that knowledge into the examination. Then do your best to pass that exam.

EXAMINATION SECTION

EXAMINATION SECTION
TEST 1

DIRECTIONS: Each question or incomplete statement is followed by several suggested answers or completions. Select the one that BEST answers the question or completes the statement. *PRINT THE LETTER OF THE CORRECT ANSWER IN THE SPACE AT THE RIGHT.*

Questions 1-6.

DIRECTIONS: Questions 1 through 6 consist of descriptions of material to which a filing designation must be assigned.

Assume that the matters and cases described in the questions were referred for handling to a government legal office which has its files set up according to these file designations. The file designation consists of a number of characters and punctuation marks as described below.

The first character refers to agencies whose legal work is handled by this office. These agencies are numbered consecutively in the order in which they first submit a matter for attention, and are identified in an alphabetical card index. To date numbers have been assigned to agencies as follows:

Department of Correction	1
Police Department	2
Department of Traffic	3
Department of Consumer Affairs	4
Commission on Human Rights	5
Board of Elections	6
Department of Personnel	7
Board of Estimate	8

The second character is separated from the first character by a dash. The second character is the last digit of the year in which a particular lawsuit or matter is referred to the legal office.

The third character is separated from the second character by a colon and may consist of either of the following:

I. A sub-number assigned to each lawsuit to which the agency is a party. Lawsuits are numbered consecutively regardless of year. (Lawsuits are brought by or against agency heads rather than agencies themselves, but references are made to agencies for the purpose of simplification.)

or II. A capital letter assigned to each matter other than a lawsuit according to subject, the subject being identified in an alphabetical index. To date, letters have been assigned to subjects as follows:

Citizenship	A	Housing	E
Discrimination	B	Gambling	F
Residence Requirements	C	Freedom of Religion	G
Civil Service Examinations	D		

These referrals are numbered consecutively regardless of year. The first referral by a particular agency on citizenship, for example, would be designated A1, followed by A2, A3, etc.

If no reference is made in a question as to how many letters involving a certain subject or how many lawsuits have been referred by an agency, assume that it is the first.

For each question, choose the file designation which is MOST appropriate for filing the material described in the question.

1. In January 2010, two candidates in a 2009 civil service examination for positions with the Department of Correction filed a suit against the Department of Personnel seeking to set aside an educational requirement for the title.
   The Department of Personnel immediately referred the lawsuit to the legal office for handling.

   A. 1-9:1   B. 1-0:D1   C. 7-9:D1   D. 7-0:1

2. In 2014, the Police Department made its sixth request for an opinion on whether an employee assignment proposed for 2015 could be considered discriminatory.

   A. 2-5:1-B6   B. 2-4:6   C. 2-4:1-B6   D. 2-4:B6

3. In 2015, a lawsuit was brought by the Bay Island Action Committee against the Board of Estimate in which the plaintiff sought withdrawal of approval of housing for the elderly in the Bay Island area given by the Board in 2015.

   A. 8-3:1   B. 8-5:1   C. 8-3:B1   D. 8-5:E1

4. In December 2014, community leaders asked the Police Department to ban outdoor meetings of a religious group on the grounds that the meetings were disrupting the area. Such meetings had been held from time to time during 2014. On January 31, 2015, the Police Department asked the government legal office for an opinion on whether granting this request would violate the worshippers' right to freedom of religion.

   A. 2-4:G-1   B. 2-5:G1   C. 2-5:B-1   D. 2-4:B1

5. In 2014, a woman filed suit against the Board of Elections. She alleged that she had not been permitted to vote at her usual polling place in the 2013 election and had been told she was not registered there. She claimed that she had always voted there and that her record card had been lost. This was the fourth case of its type for this agency.

   A. 6-4:4   B. 6-3:C4   C. 3-4:6   D. 6-3:4

6. A lawsuit was brought in 2011 by the Ace Pinball Machine Company against the Commissioner of Consumer Affairs. The lawsuit contested an ordinance which banned the use of pinball machines on the ground that they are gambling devices.
   This was the third lawsuit to which the Department of Consumer Affairs was a party.

   A. 4-1:1   B. 4-3:F1   C. 4-1:3   D. 3F-4:1

7. You are instructed by your supervisor to type a statement that must be signed by the person making the statement and by three witnesses to the signature. The typed statement will take two pages and will leave no room for signatures if the normal margin is maintained at the bottom of the second page.
   In this situation, the PREFERRED method is to type

   A. the signature lines below the normal margin on the second page
   B. nothing further and have the witnesses sign without a typed signature line
   C. the signature lines on a third page
   D. some of the text and the signature lines on a third page

8. Certain legal documents always begin with a statement of venue - that is, the county and state in which the document is executed. This is usually boxed with a parentheses or colons.
   The one of the following documents that ALWAYS bears a statement of venue in a prominent position at its head is a(n)

   A. affidavit   B. memorandum of law
   C. contract of sale   D. will

9. A court stenographer is to take stenographic notes and transcribe the statements of a person under oath. The person has a heavy accent and speaks in ungrammatical and broken English.
   When he or she is transcribing the testimony, of the following, the BEST thing for them to do is to

   A. transcribe the testimony exactly as spoken, making no grammatical changes
   B. make only the grammatical changes which would clarify the client's statements
   C. make all grammatical changes so that the testimony is in standard English form
   D. ask the client's permission before making any grammatical changes

10. When the material typed on a printed form does not fill the space provided, a Z-ruling is frequently drawn to fill up the unused space.
    The MAIN purpose of this practice is to

    A. make the document more pleasing to the eye
    B. indicate that the preceding material is correct
    C. insure that the document is not altered
    D. show that the lawyer has read it

11. After you had typed an original and five copies of a certain document, some changes were made in ink on the original and were initialed by all the parties. The original was signed by all the parties, and the signatures were notarized.
    Which of the following should *generally* be typed on the copies BEFORE filing the original and the copies? The inked changes

    A. but not the signatures, initials, or notarial data
    B. the signatures and the initials but not the notarial data
    C. and the notarial data but not the signatures or initials
    D. the signatures, the initials, and the notarial data

12. The first paragraph of a noncourt agreement *generally* contains all of the following EXCEPT the

    A. specific terms of the agreement
    B. date of the agreement
    C. purpose of the agreement
    D. names of the parties involved

13. When typing an answer in a court proceeding, the place where the word ANSWER should be typed on the first page of the document is

    A. at the upper left-hand corner
    B. below the index number and to the right of the box containing the names of the parties to the action
    C. above the index number and to the right of the box containing the names of the parties to the action
    D. to the left of the names of the attorneys for the defendant

14. Which one of the following statements BEST describes the legal document called an acknowledgment?
    It is

    A. an answer to an affidavit
    B. a receipt issued by the court when a document is filed
    C. proof of service of a summons
    D. a declaration that a signature is valid

15. Suppose you typed the original and three copies of a legal document which was dictated by an attorney in your office. He has already signed the original copy, and corrections have been made on all copies.
    Regarding the copies, which one of the following procedures is the PROPER one to follow?

    A. Leave the signature line blank on the copies
    B. Ask the attorney to sign the copies
    C. Print or type the attorney's name on the signature line on the copies
    D. Sign your name to the copies followed by the attorney's initials

16. Suppose your office is defending a particular person in a court action. This person comes to the office and asks to see some of the lawyer's working papers in his file. The lawyer assigned to the case is out of the office at the time.
    You SHOULD

    A. permit him to examine his entire file as long as he does not remove any materials from it
    B. make an appointment for the caller to come back later when the lawyer will be there
    C. ask him what working papers he wants to see and show him only those papers
    D. tell him that he needs written permission from the lawyer in order to see any records

17. Suppose that you receive a phone call from an official who is annoyed about a letter from your office which she just received. The lawyer who dictated the letter is not in the office at the moment.
    Of the following, the BEST action for you to take is to

    A. explain that the lawyer is out but that you will ask the lawyer to return her call when he returns
    B. take down all of the details of her complaint and tell her that you will get back to her with an explanation
    C. refer to the proper file so that you can give her an explanation of the reasons for the letter over the phone
    D. make an appointment for her to stop by the office to speak with the lawyer

18. Suppose that you have taken dictation for an interoffice memorandum. You are asked to prepare it for distribution to four lawyers in your department whose names are given to you. You will type an original and make four copies. Which one of the following is CORRECT with regard to the typing of the lawyers' names?
    The names of all of the lawyers should appear

    A. *only* on the original
    B. on the original and each copy should have the name of one lawyer
    C. on each of the copies but not on the original
    D. on the original and on all of the copies

19. Regarding the correct typing of punctuation, the GENERALLY accepted practice is that there should be

    A. two spaces after a semi-colon
    B. one space before an apostrophe used in the body of a word
    C. no space between parentheses and the matter enclosed
    D. one space before and after a hyphen

20. Suppose you have just completed typing an original and two copies of a letter requesting information. The original is to be signed by a lawyer in your office. The first copy is for the files, and the second is to be used as a reminder to follow up.
    The PROPER time to file the file copy of the letter is

    A. after the letter has been signed and corrections have been made on the copies
    B. before you take the letter to the lawyer for his signature
    C. after a follow-up letter has been sent
    D. after a response to the letter has been received

21. A secretary in a legal office has just typed a letter. She has typed the copy distribution notation on the copies to indicate *blind copy distribution*. This *blind copy* notation shows that

    A. copies of the letter are being sent to persons that the addressee does not know
    B. copies of the letter are being sent to other persons without the addressee's knowledge
    C. a copy of the letter will be enlarged for a legally blind person
    D. a copy of the letter is being given as an extra copy to the addressee

22. Suppose that one of the attorneys in your office dictates material to you without indicating punctuation. He has asked that you give him, as soon as possible, a single copy of a rough draft to be triple-spaced so that he can make corrections.
Of the following, what is the BEST thing for you to do in this situation?

   A. Assume that no punctuation is desired in the material
   B. Insert the punctuation as you type the rough draft
   C. Transcribe the material exactly as dictated, but attach a note to the attorney stating your suggested changes
   D. Before you start to type the draft, tell the attorney you want to read back your notes so that he can indicate punctuation

23. When it is necessary to type a mailing notation such as CERTIFIED, REGISTERED, or FEDEX on an envelope, the GENERALLY accepted place to type it is

   A. directly above the address
   B. in the area below where the stamp will be affixed
   C. in the lower left-hand corner
   D. in the upper left-hand corner

24. When taking a citation of a case in shorthand, which of the following should you write FIRST if you are having difficulty keeping up with the dictation?

   A. Volume and page number   B. Title of volume
   C. Name of plaintiff   D. Name of defendant

25. All of the following abbreviations and their meanings are correctly paired EXCEPT

   A. viz. - namely   B. ibid. - refer
   C. n.b. - note well   D. q.v. - which see

KEY (CORRECT ANSWERS)

1. D	11. D
2. D	12. A
3. B	13. B
4. B	14. D
5. A	15. C
6. C	16. B
7. D	17. A
8. A	18. D
9. A	19. C
10. C	20. A

21. B
22. B
23. B
24. A
25. B

EXAMINATION SECTION
TEST 1

DIRECTIONS: Each question or incomplete statement is followed by several suggested answers or completions. Select the one that BEST answers the question or completes the statement. *PRINT THE LETTER OF THE CORRECT ANSWER IN THE SPACE AT THE RIGHT.*

Questions 1-9.

DIRECTIONS: Questions 1 through 9 consist of sentences which may or may not be examples of good English usage. Consider grammar, punctuation, spelling, capitalization, awkwardness, etc. Examine each sentence, and then choose the correct statement about it from the four choices below it. If the English usage in the sentence given is better than it would be with any of the changes suggested in options B, C, and D, choose option A. Do not choose an option that will change the meaning of the sentence.

1. According to Judge Frank, the grocer's sons found guilty of assault and sentenced last Thursday.

    A. This is an example of acceptable writing.
    B. A comma should be placed after the word *sentenced*.
    C. The word *were* should be placed after *sons*
    D. The apostrophe in *grocer's* should be placed after the *s*.

2. The department heads assistant said that the stenographers should type duplicate copies of all contracts, leases, and bills.

    A. This is an example of acceptable writing.
    B. A comma should be placed before the word *contracts*.
    C. An apostrophe should be placed before the *s* in *heads*.
    D. Quotation marks should be placed before *the stenographers* and after *bills*.

3. The lawyers questioned the men to determine who was the true property owner?

    A. This is an example of acceptable writing.
    B. The phrase *questioned the men* should be changed to *asked the men questions*.
    C. The word *was* should be changed to *were*.
    D. The question mark should be changed to a period.

4. The terms stated in the present contract are more specific than those stated in the previous contract.

    A. This is an example of acceptable writing.
    B. The word *are* should be changed to *is*.
    C. The word *than* should be changed to *then*.
    D. The word *specific* should be changed to *specified*.

5. Of the lawyers considered, the one who argued more skillful was chosen for the job.

    A. This is an example of acceptable writing.
    B. The word *more* should be replaced by the word *most*.
    C. The word *skillful* should be replaced by the word *skillfully,*
    D. The word *chosen* should be replaced by the word *selected*.

1.____

2.____

3.____

4.____

5.____

6. Each of the states has a court of appeals; some states have circuit courts. 6._____

   A. This is an example of acceptable writing.
   B. The semi-colon should be changed to a comma.
   C. The word *has* should be changed to *have*.
   D. The word *some* should be capitalized.

7. The court trial has greatly effected the child's mental condition. 7._____

   A. This is an example of acceptable writing.
   B. The word *effected* should be changed to *affected*.
   C. The word *greatly* should be placed after *effected*.
   D. The apostrophe in *child's* should be placed after the *s*.

8. Last week, the petition signed by all the officers was sent to the Better Business Bureau. 8._____

   A. This is an example of acceptable writing.
   B. The phrase *last week* should be placed after *officers*.
   C. A comma should be placed after *petition*.
   D. The word *was* should be changed to *were*.

9. Mr. Farrell claims that he requested form A-12, and three booklets describing court procedures. 9._____

   A. This is an example of acceptable writing.
   B. The word *that* should be eliminated.
   C. A colon should be placed after *requested*.
   D. The comma after *A-12* should be eliminated.

Questions 10-21.

DIRECTIONS: Questions 10 through 21 contain a word in capital letters followed by four suggested meanings of the word. For each question, choose the BEST meaning for the word in capital letters.

10. SIGNATORY - A 10._____

    A. lawyer who draws up a legal document
    B. document that must be signed by a judge
    C. person who signs a document
    D. true copy of a signature

11. RETAINER - A 11._____

    A. fee paid to a lawyer for his services
    B. document held by a third party
    C. court decision to send a prisoner back to custody pending trial
    D. legal requirement to keep certain types of files

12. BEQUEATH - To 12._____

    A. receive assistance from a charitable organization
    B. give personal property by will to another
    C. transfer real property from one person to another
    D. receive an inheritance upon the death of a relative

13. RATIFY - To 13._____
    A. approve and sanction
    B. forego
    C. produce evidence
    D. summarize

14. CODICIL - A 14._____
    A. document introduced in evidence in a civil action
    B. subsection of a law
    C. type of legal action that can be brought by a plaintiff
    D. supplement or an addition to a will

15. ALIAS 15._____
    A. Assumed name
    B. In favor of
    C. Against
    D. A writ

16. PROXY - A(n) 16._____
    A. phony document in a real estate transaction
    B. opinion by a judge of a civil court
    C. document containing appointment of an agent
    D. summons in a lawsuit

17. ALLEGED 17._____
    A. Innocent
    B. Asserted
    C. Guilty
    D. Called upon

18. EXECUTE - To 18._____
    A. complete a legal document by signing it
    B. set requirements
    C. render services to a duly elected executive of a municipality
    D. initiate legal action such as a lawsuit

19. NOTARY PUBLIC - A 19._____
    A. lawyer who is running for public office
    B. judge who hears minor cases
    C. public officer, one of whose functions is to administer oaths
    D. lawyer who gives free legal services to persons unable to pay

20. WAIVE - To 20._____
    A. disturb a calm state of affairs
    B. knowingly renounce a right or claim
    C. pardon someone for a minor fault
    D. purposely mislead a person during an investigation

21. ARRAIGN - To 21._____
    A. prevent an escape
    B. defend a prisoner
    C. verify a document
    D. accuse in a court of law

Questions 22-40.

DIRECTIONS: Questions 22 through 40 each consist of four words which may or may not be spelled correctly. If you find an error in
only one word, mark your answer A;
any two words, mark your answer B;
any three words, mark your answer C;
none of these words, mark your answer D.

22.	occurrence	Febuary	privilege	similiar	22._____
23.	separate	transferring	analyze	column	23._____
24.	develop	license	bankrupcy	abreviate	24._____
25.	subpoena	arguement	dissolution	foreclosure	25._____
26.	exaggerate	fundamental	significance	warrant	26._____
27.	citizen	endorsed	marraige	appraissal	27._____
28.	precedant	univercity	observence	preliminary	28._____
29.	stipulate	negligence	judgment	prominent	29._____
30.	judisial	whereas	release	guardian	30._____
31.	appeal	larcenny	transcrip	jurist	31._____
32.	petition	tenancy	agenda	insurance	32._____
33.	superfical	premise	morgaged	maintainance	33._____
34.	testamony	publically	installment	possessed	34._____
35.	escrow	decree	eviction	miscelaneous	35._____
36.	securitys	abeyance	adhere	corporate	36._____
37.	kaleidoscope	anesthesia	vermilion	tafetta	37._____
38.	congruant	barrenness	plebescite	vigilance	38._____
39.	picnicing	promisory	resevoir	omission	39._____
40.	supersede	banister	wholly	seize	40._____

KEY (CORRECT ANSWERS)

1. C	11. A	21. D	31. B
2. C	12. B	22. B	32. D
3. D	13. A	23. D	33. C
4. A	14. D	24. B	34. B
5. C	15. A	25. A	35. A
6. A	16. C	26. D	36. A
7. B	17. B	27. B	37. A
8. A	18. A	28. C	38. B
9. D	19. C	29. D	39. C
10. C	20. B	30. A	40. D

EXAMINATION SECTION
TEST 1

DIRECTIONS: Each question or incomplete statement is followed by several suggested answers or completions. Select the one that BEST answers the question or completes the statement. *PRINT THE LETTER OF THE CORRECT ANSWER IN THE SPACE AT THE RIGHT.*

Questions 1-10.

WORD MEANING

DIRECTIONS: Each question from 1 to 10 contains a word in capitals followed by four suggested meanings of the word. For each question, choose the best meaning. *PRINT THE LETTER OF THE CORRECT ANSWER IN THE SPACE AT THE RIGHT.*

1. ACCURATE
    A. correct   B. useful   C. afraid   D. careless

2. ALTER
    A. copy   B. change   C. report   D. agree

3. DOCUMENT
    A. outline   B. agreement   C. blueprint   D. record

4. INDICATE
    A. listen   B. show   C. guess   D. try

5. INVENTORY
    A. custom   B. discovery   C. warning   D. list

6. ISSUE
    A. annoy   B. use up   C. give out   D. gain

7. NOTIFY
    A. inform   B. promise   C. approve   D. strengthen

8. ROUTINE
    A. path   B. mistake   C. habit   D. journey

9. TERMINATE
    A. rest   B. start   C. deny   D. end

10. TRANSMIT
    A. put in   B. send   C. stop   D. go across

Questions 11-15.

READING COMPREHENSION

DIRECTIONS: Questions 11 through 15 test how well you understand what you read. It will be necessary for you to read carefully because your answers to these questions should be based ONLY on the information given in the following paragraphs.

The recipient gains an impression of a typewritten letter before he begins to read the message. Pastors which provide for a good first impression include margins and spacing that are visually pleasing, formal parts of the letter which are correctly placed according to the style of the letter, copy which is free of obvious erasures and over-strikes, and transcript that is even and clear. The problem for the typist is that of how to produce that first, positive impression of her work.

There are several general rules which a typist can follow when she wishes to prepare a properly spaced letter on a sheet of letter-head. Ordinarily, the width of a letter should not be less than four inches nor more than six inches. The side margins should also have a desirable relation to the bottom margin and the space between the letterhead and the body of the letter. Usually the most appealing arrangement is when the side margins are even and the bottom margin is slightly wider than the side margins. In some offices, however, standard line length is used for all business letters, and the secretary then varies the spacing between the date line and the inside address according to the length of the letter.

11. The BEST title for the above paragraphs would be: 11.____

    A. Writing Office Letters
    B. Making Good First Impressions
    C. Judging Well-Typed Letters
    D. Good Placing and Spacing for Office Letters

12. According to the above paragraphs, which of the following might be considered the way in which people very quickly judge the quality of work which has been typed? By 12.____

    A. measuring the margins to see if they are correct
    B. looking at the spacing and cleanliness of the typescript
    C. scanning the body of the letter for meaning
    D. reading the date line and address for errors

13. What, according to the above paragraphs, would be definitely UNDESIRABLE as the average line length of a typed letter? 13.____

    A. 4"   B. 5"   C. 6"   D. 7"

14. According to the above paragraphs, when the line length is kept standard, the secretary 14.____

    A. does not have to vary the spacing at all since this also is standard
    B. adjusts the spacing between the date line and inside address for different lengths of letters
    C. uses the longest line as a guideline for spacing between the date line and inside address
    D. varies the number of spaces between the lines

15. According to the above paragraphs, side margins are MOST pleasing when they 15.____
   A. are even and somewhat smaller than the bottom margin
   B. are slightly wider than the bottom margin
   C. vary with the length of the letter
   D. are figured independently from the letterhead and the body of the letter

Questions 16-20.

CODING

DIRECTIONS:

Name of Applicant	H A N G S B R U K E
Test Code	c o m p l e x i t y
File Number	0 1 2 3 4 5 6 7 8 9

Assume that each of the above capital letters is the first letter of the name of an Applicant, that the small letter directly beneath each capital letter is the test code for the Applicant, and that the number directly beneath each code letter is the file number for the Applicant.

In each of the following Questions 16 through 20, the test code letters and the file numbers in Columns 2 and 3 should correspond to the capital letters in Column 1. For each question, look at each column carefully and mark your answer as follows:

If there is an error only in Column 2, mark your answer A.
If there is an error only in Column 3, mark your answer B.
If there is an error in both Columns 2 and 3, mark your answer C.
If both Columns 2 and 3 are correct, mark your answer D.

The following sample question is given to help you understand the procedure.

SAMPLE QUESTION

Column 1	Column 2	Column 3
AKEHN	otyci	18902

In Column 2, the final test code letter *i.* should be *m*. Column 3 is correctly coded to Column 1. Since there is an error only in Column 2, the answer is A.

	Column 1	Column 2	Column 3	
16.	NEKKU	mytti	29987	16.____
17.	KRAEB	txyle	86095	17.____
18.	ENAUK	ymoit	92178	18.____
19.	REANA	xeomo	69121	19.____
20.	EKHSE	ytcxy	97049	20.____

Questions 21-30.

ARITHMETICAL REASONING

21. If a secretary answered 28 phone calls and typed the addresses for 112 credit statements in one morning, what is the ratio of phone calls answered to credit statements typed for that period of time?

    A. 1:4 B. 1:7 C. 2:3 D. 3:5

22. According to a suggested filing system, no more than 10 folders should be filed behind any one file guide and from 15 to 25 file guides should be used in each file drawer for easy finding and filing.
    The maximum number of folders that a five-drawer file cabinet can hold to allow easy finding and filing is

    A. 550 B. 750 C. 1,100 D. 1,250

23. An employee had a starting salary of $25,804. He received a salary increase at the end of each year, and at the end of the seventh year his salary was $33,476.
    What was his average annual increase in salary over these seven years?

    A. $1,020 B. $1,076 C. $1,096 D. $1,144

24. The 55 typists and 28 senior clerks in a certain city agency were paid a total of $1,943,200 in salaries last year.
    If the average annual salary of a typist was $22,400 the average annual salary of a senior clerk was

    A. $25,400 B. $26,600 C. $26,800 D. $27,000

25. A typist has been given a three page report to type. She has finished typing the first two pages. The first page has 283 words, and the second page has 366 words.
    If the total report consists of 954 words, how many words will she have to type on the third page of the report?

    A. 202 B. 287 C. 305 D. 313

26. In one day, Clerk A processed 30% more forms than Clerk B, and Clerk C processed 1¼ times as many forms as Clerk A. If Clerk B processed 40 forms, how many more forms were processed by Clerk C than Clerk B?

    A. 12 B. 13 C. 21 D. 25

27. A clerk who earns a gross salary of $452 every two weeks has the following deductions taken from her paycheck:
    15% for City, State, Federal taxes; 2 1/2% for Social Security; $1.30 for health insurance; and $6.00 for union dues. The amount of her take-home pay is

    A. $256.20 B. $312.40 C. $331.60 D. $365.60

28. In 2005, a city agency spent $2,000 to buy pencils at a cost of $5.00 a dozen.
    If the agency used 3/4 of these pencils in 2005 and used the same number of pencils in 2006, how many more pencils did it have to buy to have enough pencils for all of 2006?

    A. 1,200 B. 2,400 C. 3,600 D. 4,800

29. A clerk who worked in Agency X earned the following salaries: $20,140 the first year, $21,000 the second year, and $21,920 the third year. Another clerk who worked in Agency Y for three years earned $21,100 a year for two years and $21,448 the third year. The difference between the average salaries received by both clerks over a three-year period is

    A. $196 B. $204 C. $348 D. $564

30. An employee who works over 40 hours in any week receives overtime payment for the extra hours at time and one-half (1 1/2 times) his hourly rate of pay. An employee who earns $13.60 an hour works a total of 45 hours during a certain week.
    His total pay for that week would be

    A. $564.40 B. $612.00 C. $646.00 D. $812.00

Questions 31-35.

RELATED INFORMATION

31. To tell a newly-employed clerk to fill a top drawer of a four-drawer cabinet with heavy folders which will be often used and to keep lower drawers only partly filled is

    A. *good,* because a tall person would have to bend unnecessarily if he had to use a lower drawer
    B. *bad,* because the file cabinet may tip over when the top drawer is opened
    C. *good,* because it is the most easily reachable drawer for the average person
    D. *bad,* because a person bending down at another drawer may accidentally bang his head on the bottom of the drawer when he straightens up

32. If a senior typist or senior clerk has requisitioned a *ream* of paper in order to duplicate a single page office announcement, how many announcements can be printed from the one package of paper?

    A. 200 B. 500 C. 700 D. 1,000

33. Your supervisor has asked you to locate a telephone number for an attorney named Jones, whose office is located at 311 Broadway, and whose name is not already listed in your files.
    The BEST method for finding the number would be for you to

    A. call the information operator and have her get it for you
    B. look in the alphabetical directory (white pages) under the name Jones at 311 Broadway
    C. refer to the heading Attorney in the yellow pages for the name Jones at 311 Broadway
    D. ask your supervisor who referred her to Mr. Jones, then call that person for the number

34. An example of material that should NOT be sent by first class mail is a

    A. email copy of a letter   B. post card
    C. business reply card   D. large catalogue

35. In the operations of a government agency, a voucher is ORDINARILY used to

    A. refer someone to the agency for a position or assignment
    B. certify that an agency's records of financial trans-actions are accurate
    C. order payment from agency funds of a stated amount to an individual
    D. enter a statement of official opinion in the records of the agency

35.____

Questions 36-40.

ENGLISH USAGE

DIRECTIONS: Each question from 36 through 40 contains a sentence. Read each sentence carefully to decide whether it is correct. Then, in the space at the right, mark your answer:

(A) if the sentence is incorrect because of bad grammar or sentence structure

(B) if the sentence is incorrect because of bad punctuation

(C) if the sentence is incorrect because of bad capitalization

(D) if the sentence is correct

Each incorrect sentence has only one type of error. Consider a sentence correct if it has no errors, although there may be other correct ways of saying the same thing.

SAMPLE QUESTION I: One of our clerks were promoted yesterday.

The subject of this sentence is *one,* so the verb should be *was promoted* instead of *were promoted.* Since the sentence is incorrect because of bad grammar, the answer to Sample Question I is (A).

SAMPLE QUESTION II: Between you and me, I would prefer not going there.

Since this sentence is correct, the answer to Sample Question II is (D).

36. The National alliance of Businessmen is trying to persuade private businesses to hire youth in the summertime.

36.____

37. The supervisor who is on vacation, is in charge of processing vouchers.

37.____

38. The activity of the committee at its conferences is always stimulating.

38.____

39. After checking the addresses again, the letters went to the mailroom.

39.____

40. The director, as well as the employees, are interested in sharing the dividends.

40.____

Questions 41-45.

FILING

DIRECTIONS: Each question from 41 through 45 contains four names. For each question, choose the name that should be FIRST if the four names are to be arranged in alphabeti-cal order in accordance with the Rules for Alphabetical Filing given below. Read these rules carefully. Then, for each question, indicate in the space at the right the letter before the name that should be FIRST in alphabet-ical order.

RULES FOR ALPHABETICAL FILING

Names of People

(1) The names of people are filed in strict alphabetical order, first according to the last name, then according to first name or initial, and finally according to middle name or initial. FOR EXAMPLE: George Allen comes before Edward Bell, and Leonard P. Reston comes before Lucille B. Reston.

(2) When last names are the same, FOR EXAMPLE, A. Green and Agnes Green, the one with the initial comes before the one with the name written out when the first initials are identi-cal.

(3) When first and last names are alike and the middle name is given, FOR EXAMPLE, John David Doe and John Devoe Doe, the names should be filed in the alphabetical order of the middle names.

(4) When first and last names are the same, a name without a middle initial comes before one with a middle name or initial. FOR EXAMPLE, John Doe comes before both John A. Doe and John Alan Doe.

(5) When first and last names are the same, a name with a middle initial comes before one with a middle name beginning with the same initial. FOR EXAMPLE: Jack R. Hertz comes before Jack Richard Hertz.

(6) Prefixes such as De, O', Mac, Mc, and Van are filed as written and are treated as part of the names to which they are connected. FOR EXAMPLE: Robert O'Dea is filed before David Olsen.

(7) Abbreviated names are treated as if they were spelled out. FOR EXAMPLE: Chas. is filed as Charles and Thos. is filed as Thomas.

(8) Titles and designations such as Dr., Mr., and Prof, are disregarded in filing.

Names of Organizations

(1) The names of business organizations are filed according to the order in which each word in the name appears. When an organization name bears the name of a person, it is filed according to the rules for filing names of people as given above. FOR EXAMPLE: William Smith Service Co. comes before Television Distributors, Inc.

(2) Where bureau, board, office, or department appears as the first part of the title of a governmental agency, that agency should be filed under the word in the title expressing the chief function of the agency. FOR EXAMPLE: Bureau of the Budget would be filed as if written Budget, (Bureau of the). The Department of Personnel would be filed as if written Personnel, (Department of).

(3) When the following words are part of an organization, they are disregarded: the, of, and.

(4) When there are numbers in a name, they are treated as if they were spelled out. FOR EXAMPLE: 10th Street Bootery is filed as Tenth Street Bootery.

SAMPLE QUESTION:
- A. Jane Earl (2)
- B. James A. Earle (4)
- C. James Earl (1)
- D. J. Earle (3)

The numbers in parentheses show the proper alphabetical order in which these names should be filed. Since the name that should be filed FIRST is James Earl, the answer to the Sample Question is (C).

41.
- A. Majorca Leather Goods
- B. Robert Maiorca and Sons
- C. Maintenance Management Corp.
- D. Majestic Carpet Mills

42.
- A. Municipal Telephone Service
- B. Municipal Reference Library
- C. Municipal Credit Union
- D. Municipal Broadcasting System

43.
- A. Robert B. Pierce
- B. R. Bruce Pierce
- C. Ronald Pierce
- D. Robert Bruce Pierce

44.
- A. Four Seasons Sports Club
- B. 14th. St. Shopping Center
- C. Forty Thieves Restaurant
- D. 42nd St. Theaters

45.
- A. Franco Franceschini
- B. Amos Franchini
- C. Sandra Franceschia
- D. Lilie Franchinesca

Questions 46-50.

SPELLING

DIRECTIONS: In each question, one of the words is misspelled. Select the letter of the misspelled word. *PRINT THE LETTER OF THE CORRECT ANSWER IN THE SPACE AT THE RIGHT.*

46.
- A. option
- B. extradite
- C. comparitive
- D. jealousy

47.
- A. handicaped
- B. assurance
- C. sympathy
- D. speech

48. A. recommend B. carraige 48._____
    C. disapprove D. independent

49. A. ingenuity   B. tenet (opinion) 49._____
    C. uncanny   D. intrigueing

50. A. arduous   B. hideous 50._____
    C. iervant   D. companies

KEY (CORRECT ANSWERS)

1. A	11. D	21. A	31. B	41. C
2. B	12. B	22. D	32. B	42. D
3. D	13. D	23. C	33. C	43. B
4. B	14. B	24. A	34. D	44. D
5. D	15. A	25. C	35. C	45. C
6. C	16. B	26. D	36. C	46. C
7. A	17. C	27. D	37. B	47. A
8. C	18. D	28. B	38. D	48. B
9. D	19. A	29. A	39. A	49. D
10. B	20. C	30. C	40. A	50. C'

EXAMINATION SECTION
TEST 1

DIRECTIONS: Each question or incomplete statement is followed by several suggested answers or completions. Select the one that BEST answers the question or completes the statement. *PRINT THE LETTER OF THE CORRECT ANSWER IN THE SPACE AT THE RIGHT.*

1. A multi-line telephone with buttons for eight separate lines, plus a *hold* button, is often used when an office requires more than one outside line.
   If you are talking on one line of this type of office phone when another call comes in, what is the procedure to follow if you want to answer the second call but keep the first call on the line?
   Push the
   A. *hold* button at the same time as you push the *pickup* button of the ringing line
   B. *hold* button and then push the *pickup* button of the ringing line
   C. *pickup* button of the ringing line and then push the *hold* button
   D. *pickup* button of the ringing line and push the *hold* button when you return to the original line

   1._____

2. Suppose that you are asked to prepare a petty cash statement for March. The original and one copy are to go to the personnel office. One copy is to go to the fiscal office, and another copy is to go to your supervisor. The last copy is for your files.
   In preparing the statement and the copies, how many sheets of copy paper should you use?
   A. 3 B. 4 C. 5 D. 8

   2._____

3. Which one of the following is the LEAST important advantage of putting the subject of a letter in the heading to the right of the address? It
   A. makes filing of the copy easier
   B. makes more space available in the body of the letter
   C. simplifies distribution of letters
   D. simplifies determination of the subject of the letter

   3._____

4. Of the following, the MOST efficient way to put 100 copies of a one-page letter into 9½" x 4⅛" envelopes for mailing is to fold _____ into an envelope.
   A. each letter and insert it immediately after folding
   B. each letter separately until all 100 are folded; then insert each one
   C. the 100 letters two at a time, then separate them and insert each one
   D. two letters together, slip them apart, and insert each one

   4._____

5. When preparing papers for filing, it is NOT desirable to
   A. smooth papers that are wrinkled
   B. use paper clips to keep related papers together in the files
   C. arrange the papers in the order in which they will be filed
   D. mend torn papers with cellophane tape

6. Of the following, the BEST reason for a clerical unit to have its own duplicating machine is that the unit
   A. uses many forms which it must reproduce internally
   B. must make two copies of each piece of incoming mail for a special file
   C. must make seven copies of each piece of outgoing mail
   D. must type 200 envelopes each month for distribution to the same offices

7. Several offices use the same photocopying machine.
   If each office must pay its share of the cost of running this machine, the BEST way of determining how much of this cost should be charged to each of these offices is to
   A. determine the monthly number of photocopies made by each office
   B. determine the monthly number of originals submitted for photocopying by each office
   C. determine the number of times per day each office uses the photocopying machine
   D. divide the total cost of running the photocopy machine by the total number of offices using the machine

8. Which one of the following would it be BEST to use to indicate that a file folder has been removed from the files for temporary use in another office?
   A(n)
   A. cross-reference card   B. tickler file marker
   C. aperture card   D. out guide

9. Which one of the following is the MOST important objective of filing?
   A. Giving a secretary something to do in her spare time
   B. Making it possible to locate information quickly
   C. Providing a place to store unneeded documents
   D. Keeping extra papers from accumulating on workers' desks

10. If a check has been made out for an incorrect amount, the BEST action for the writer of the check to take is to
    A. erase the original amount and enter the correct amount
    B. cross out the original amount with a single line and enter the correct amount above it
    C. black out the original amount so that it cannot be read and enter the correct amount above it
    D. write a new check

11. Which one of the following BEST describes the usual arrangement of a tickler file?
    A. Alphabetical
    B. Chronological
    C. Numerical
    D. Geographical

    11._____

12. Which one of the following is the LEAST desirable filing practice?
    A. Using staples to keep papers together
    B. Filing all material without regard to date
    C. Keeping a record of all materials removed from the files
    D. Writing filing instructions on each paper prior to filing

    12._____

13. Assume that one of your duties is to keep records of the office supplies used by your unit for the purpose of ordering new supplies when the old supplies run out.
    The information that will be of MOST help in letting you know when to reorder supplies is the
    A. quantity issued
    B. quantity received
    C. quantity on hand
    D. stock number

    13._____

Questions 14-19.

DIRECTIONS: Questions 14 through 19 consist of sets of names and addresses. In each question, the name and address in Column II should be an exact copy of the name and address in Column I. If there is
a mistake *only* in the name, mark your answer A;
a mistake *only* in the address, mark your answer B;
a mistake in *both* name and address, mark your answer C;
no mistake in either name or address, mark your answer D.

SAMPLE QUESTION

Column I
Michael Filbert
456 Reade Street
New York, N.Y. 10013

Column II
Michael Filbert
645 Reade Street
New York, N.Y. 10013

Since there is a mistake only in the address (the street number should be 456 instead of 645), the answer to the sample question is B.

COLUMN I

COLUMN II

14. Esta Wong
    141 West 68 St.
    New York, N.Y. 10023

    Esta Wang
    141 West 68 St.
    New York,, N.Y. 10023

    14._____

15. Dr. Alberto Grosso
    3475 12th Avenue
    Brooklyn, N.Y. 11218

    Dr. Alberto Grosso
    3475 12th Avenue
    Brooklyn, N.Y. 11218

    15._____

	Column I	Column II	
16.	Mrs. Ruth Bortlas 482 Theresa Ct. Far Rockaway, N.Y. 11691	Ms. Ruth Bortlas 482 Theresa Ct. Far Rockaway, N.Y. 11169	16.____
17.	Mr. and Mrs. Howard Fox 2301 Sedgwick Avenue Bronx, N.Y. 10468	Mr. and Mrs. Howard Fox 231 Sedgwick Ave. Bronx, N.Y. 10458	17.____
18.	Miss Marjorie Black 223 East 23 Street New York, N.Y. 10010	Miss Margorie Black 223 East 23 Street New York, N.Y. 10010	18.____
19.	Michelle Herman 806 Valley Rd. Old Tappan, N.J. 07675	Michelle Hermann 806 Valley Dr. Old Tappan, N.J. 07675	19.____

Questions 20-25.

DIRECTIONS: Questions 20 through 25 are to be answered SOLELY on the basis of the information in the following passage.

Basic to every office is the need for proper lighting. Inadequate lighting is a familiar cause of fatigue and serves to create a somewhat dismal atmosphere in the office. One requirement of proper lighting is that it be of an appropriate intensity. Intensity is measured in foot-candles. According to the Illuminating Engineering Society of New York, for casual seeing tasks such as in reception rooms, inactive file rooms, and other service areas, it is recommended that the amount of light be 30 foot-candles. For ordinary seeing tasks such as reading and work in active file rooms and in mail rooms, the recommended lighting is 100 foot-candles. For very difficult seeing tasks such as accounting, transcribing, and business machine use, the recommended lighting is 150 foot-candles.

Lighting intensity is only one requirement. Shadows and glare are to be avoided. For example, the larger the proportion of a ceiling filled with lighting units, the more glare-free and comfortable the lighting will be. Natural lighting from windows is not too dependable because on dark wintry days, windows yield little usable light, and on sunny afternoons, the glare from windows may be very distracting. Desks should not face the windows. Finally, the main lighting source ought to be overhead and to the left of the user.

20. According to the above passage, insufficient light in the office may cause　　　　20.____
　　A. glare　　　　B. shadows　　　C. tiredness　　D. distraction

21. Based on the above passage, which of the following must be considered when　　21.____
　　planning lighting arrangements?
　　The
　　A. amount of natural light present
　　B. amount of work to be done
　　C. level of difficulty of work to be done
　　D. type of activity to be carried out

22. It can be inferred from the above passage that a well-coordinated lighting scheme is LIKELY to result in
    A. greater employee productivity
    B. elimination of light reflection
    C. lower lighting cost
    D. more use of natural light

23. Of the following, the BEST title for the above passage is
    A. Characteristics of Light
    B. Light Measurement Devices
    C. Factors to Consider When Planning Lighting Systems
    D. Comfort vs. Cost When Devising Lighting Arrangements

24. According to the above passage, a foot-candle is a measurement of the
    A. number of bulbs used
    B. strength of the light
    C. contrast between glare and shadow
    D. proportion of the ceiling filled with lighting units

25. According to the above passage, the number of foot-candles of light that would be needed to copy figures onto a payroll is _____ foot-candles.
    A. less than 30
    B. 30
    C. 100
    D. 150

KEY (CORRECT ANSWERS)

1.	B	11.	B
2.	B	12.	B
3.	B	13.	C
4.	A	14.	A
5.	B	15.	D
6.	A	16.	C
7.	A	17.	B
8.	D	18.	A
9.	B	19.	C
10.	D	20.	C

21. D
22. A
23. C
24. B
25. D

TEST 2

DIRECTIONS: Each question or incomplete statement is followed by several suggested answers or completions. Select the one that BEST answers the question or completes the statement. *PRINT THE LETTER OF THE CORRECT ANSWER IN THE SPACE AT THE RIGHT.*

1. Assume that a supervisor has three subordinates who perform clerical tasks. One of the employees retires and is replaced by someone who is transferred from another unit in the agency. The transferred employee tells the supervisor that she has worked as a clerical employee for two years and understands clerical operations quite well. The supervisor then assigns the transferred employee to a desk, tells the employee to begin working, and returns to his own desk.
   The supervisor's action in this situation is
   A. *proper;* experienced clerical employees do not require training when they are transferred to new assignments
   B. *improper;* before the supervisor returns to his desk, he should tell the other two subordinates to watch the transferred employee perform the work
   C. *proper;* if the transferred employee makes any mistakes, she will bring them to the supervisor's attention
   D. *improper;* the supervisor should find out what clerical tasks the transferred employee has performed and give her instruction in those which are new or different

1.____

2. Assume that you are falling behind in completing your work assignments and you believe that your workload is too heavy.
   Of the following, the BEST course of action for you to take FIRST is to
   A. discuss the problem with your supervisor
   B. decide which of your assignments can be postponed
   C. try to get some of your co-workers to help you out
   D. plan to take some of the work home with you in order to catch up

2.____

3. Suppose that one of the clerks under your supervision is filling in monthly personnel forms. She asks you to explain a particular personnel regulation which is related to various items on the forms. You are not thoroughly familiar with the regulation.
   Of the following responses you may make, the one which will gain the MOST respect from the clerk and which is generally the MOST advisable is to
   A. tell the clerk to do the best she can and that you will check her work later
   B. inform the clerk that you are not sure of a correct explanation but suggest a procedure for her to follow
   C. give the clerk a suitable interpretation so that she will think you are familiar with all regulations
   D. tell the clerk that you will have to read the regulation more thoroughly before you can give her an explanation

3.____

4. Charging out records until a specified due date, with prompt follow-up if they are not returned, is a
   A. *good* idea; it may prevent the records from being kept needlessly on someone's desk for long periods of time
   B. *good* idea; it will indicate the extent of your authority to other departments
   C. *poor* idea; the person borrowing the material may make an error because of the pressure put upon him to return the records
   D. *poor* idea; other departments will feel that you do not trust them with the records and they will be resentful

Questions 5-9.

DIRECTIONS: Questions 5 through 9 consist of three lines of code letters and numbers. The numbers on each line should correspond with the code letters on the same line in accordance with the table below.

Code Letter	P	L	I	J	B	O	H	U	C	G
Corresponding Letter	0	1	2	3	4	5	6	7	8	9

On some of the lines, an error exists in the coding. Compare the letters and numbers in each question carefully. If you find an error or errors on
 only one of the lines in the question, mark your answer A;
 any two lines in the question, mark your answer B;
 all three lines in the question, mark your answer C;
 none of the lines in the question, mark your answer D.

SAMPLE QUESTION
JHOILCP   3652180
BICLGUP   4286970
UCIBHLJ   5824613

In the above sample, the first line is correct since each code letter listed has the correct corresponding number. On the second line, an error exists because code letter L should have the number 1 instead of the number 6. On the third line, an error exists because the code letter U should have the number 7 instead of the number 5. Since there are errors on two of the three lines, the correct answer is B.

5. BULJCIP   4713920
    HIGPOUL   6290571
    OCUHJJBI 5876342

6. CUBLOIJ   8741023
    LCLGCLB   1818914
    JPUHIOC   3076158

7. OIJGCBPO 52398405
    UHPBLIOP 76041250
    CLUIPGPC 81720908

8. BPCOUOJI   40875732
    UOHCIPLB   75682014
    GLHUUCBJ   92677843

9. HOIOHJLH   65256361
    IOJJHHBP   25536640
    OJHBJOPI   53642502

Questions 10-13.

DIRECTIONS: Questions 10 through 13 are to be answered SOLELY on the basis of the information given in the following passage.

The mental attitude of the employee toward safety is exceedingly important in preventing accidents. All efforts designed to keep safety on the employee's mind and to keep accident prevention a live subject in the office will help substantially in a safety program. Although it may seem strange, it is common for people to be careless. Therefore, safety education is a continuous process.

Safety rules should be explained, and the reasons for their rigid enforcement should be given to employees. Telling employees to be careful or giving similar general safety warnings and slogans is probably of little value. Employees should be informed of basic safety fundamentals. This can be done through staff meetings, informal suggestions to employees, movies, and safety instruction cards. Safety instruction cards provide the employees with specific suggestions about safety and serve as a series of timely reminder helping to keep safety on the minds of employees. Pictures, posters, and cartoon sketches on bulletin boards that are located in areas continually used by employees arouse the employees' interest in safety. It is usually good to supplement this type of safety promotion with intensive individual follow-up.

10. The above passage implies that the LEAST effective of the following safety measures is
    A. rigid enforcement of safety rules
    B. getting employees to think in terms of safety
    C. elimination of unsafe conditions in the office
    D. telling employees to stay alert at all times

11. The reason given by the passage for maintaining ongoing safety education is that
    A. people are often careless
    B. office tasks are often dangerous
    C. the value of safety slogans increases with repetition
    D. safety rules change frequently

12. Which one of the following safety aids is MOST likely to be preferred by the passage? A
    A. cartoon of a man tripping over a carton and yelling, *Keep aisles clear!*
    B. poster with a large number one and a caption saying, *Safety First*

C. photograph of a very neatly arranged office
D. large sign with the word *THINK* in capital letters

13. Of the following, the BEST title for the above passage is
    A. Basic Safety Fundamentals
    B. Enforcing Safety Among Careless Employees
    C. Attitudes Toward Safety
    D. Making Employees Aware of Safety

Questions 14-21.

DIRECTIONS: Questions 14 through 21 are to be answered SOLELY on the basis of the information and chart given below.

The following chart shows expenses in five selected categories for a one-year period, expressed as percentages of these same expenses during the previous year. The chart compares two different offices. In Office T (represented by ▨▨▨), a cost reduction program has been tested for the past year. The other office, Office Q (represented by ▨▨▨), served as a control, in that no special effort was made to reduce costs during the past year.

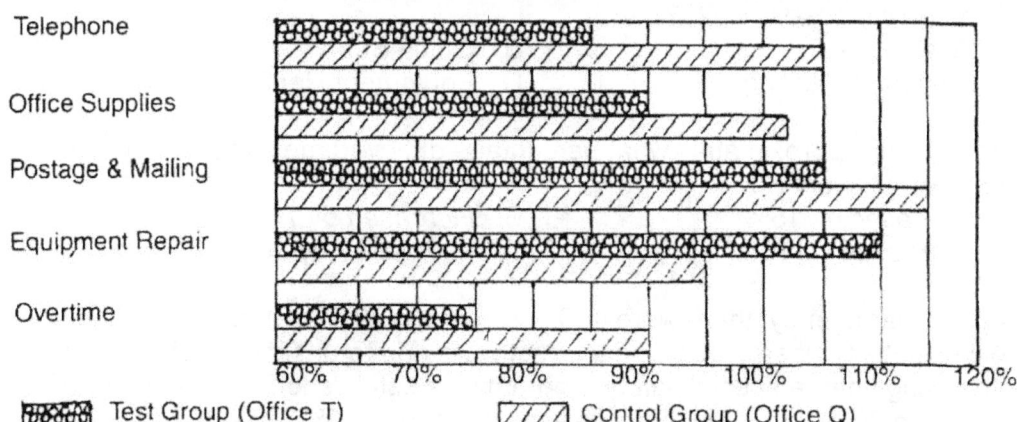

RESULTS OF OFFICE COST REDUCTION PROGRAM
Expenses of Test and Control Groups for 2020
Expressed as Percentages of Same Expenses for 2019

14. In Office T, which category of expense showed the greatest percentage REDUCTION from 2019 to 2020?
    A. Telephone
    B. Office Supplies
    C. Postage & Mailing
    D. Overtime

15. In which expense category did Office T show the BEST results in percentage terms when compared to Office Q?
    A. Telephone
    B. Office Supplies
    C. Postage & Mailing
    D. Overtime

16. According to the above chart, the cost reduction program was LEAST effective for the expense category of
    A. Office Supplies
    B. Postage & Mailing
    C. Equipment Repair
    D. Overtime

17. Office T's telephone costs went down during 2020 by approximately how many percentage points?
    A. 15   B. 20   C. 85   D. 104

18. Which of the following changes occurred in expenses for Office Supplies in Office Q in the year 2020 as compared with the year 2019? They
    A. increased by more than 100%
    B. remained the same
    C. decreased by a few percentage points
    D. increased by a few percentage points

19. For which of the following expense categories do the results in Office T and the results in Office Q differ MOST NEARLYY by 10 percentage points?
    A. Telephone
    B. Postage & Mailing
    C. Equipment Repair
    D. Overtime

20. In which expense category did Office Q's costs show the GREATEST percentage increase in 2020?
    A. Telephone
    B. Office Supplies
    C. Postage & Mailing
    D. Equipment Repair

21. In Office T, by approximately what percentage did overtime expense change during the past year? It
    A. *increased* by 15%
    B. *increased* by 75%
    C. *decreased* by 10%
    D. *decreased* by 25%

22. In a particular agency, there were 160 accidents in 2017. Of these accidents, 75% were due to unsafe acts and the rest were due to unsafe conditions. In the following year, a special safety program was established. The number of accidents in 2019 due to unsafe acts was reduced to 35% of what it had been in 2017.
    How many accidents due to unsafe acts were there in 2019?
    A. 20   B. 36   C. 42   D. 56

23. At the end of every month, the petty cash fund of Agency A is reimbursed for payments made from the fund during the month. During the month of February, the amounts paid from the fund were entered on receipts as follows: 10 bus fares of $3.50 each and one taxi fare of $35.00. At the end of the month, the money left in the fund was in the following denominations: 15 ten-dollar bills, 10 one-dollar bills, 40 quarters, and 100 dimes.
    If the petty cash fund is reduced by 20% for the following month, how much money will there be available in the petty cash fund for March?
    A. $110.00   B. $200.00   C. $215.00   D. $250.00

24. The one of the following records which it would be MOST advisable to keep in alphabetical order is a
    A. continuous listing of phone messages, including time and caller, for your supervisor
    B. listing of individuals currently employed by your agency in a particular title
    C. record of purchases paid for by the petty cash fund
    D. dated record of employees who have borrowed material from the files in your office

25. Assume that you have been asked to copy by hand a column of numbers with two decimal places from one record to another. Each number consists of three, four, and five digits.
    In order to copy them quickly and accurately, you should copy
    A. each number exactly, making sure that the column of digits farthest to the right is in a straight line and all other columns are lined up
    B. the column of digits farthest to the right and then copy the next column of digits moving from right to left
    C. the column of digits farthest to the left and then copy the next column of digits moving from left to right
    D. the digits to the right of each decimal point and then copy the digits to the left of each decimal point

KEY (CORRECT ANSWERS)

1.	D		11.	A
2.	A		12.	A
3.	D		13.	D
4.	A		14.	D
5.	A		15.	A
6.	C		16.	C
7.	D		17.	A
8.	B		18.	D
9.	C		19.	B
10.	D		20.	C

21.	D
22.	C
23.	B
24.	B
25.	A

CLERICAL ABILITIES TEST
EXAMINATION SECTION
TEST 1

DIRECTIONS: Each question or incomplete statement is followed by several suggested answers or completions. Select the one that BEST answers the question or completes the statement. *PRINT THE LETTER OF THE CORRECT ANSWER IN THE SPACE AT THE RIGHT.*

Questions 1-10.

DIRECTIONS: Questions 1 through 10 consist of lines of names, dates, and numbers. For each question, you are to choose the option (A, B, C, or D) in Column II which EXACTLY matches the information in Column I. *PRINT THE LETTER OF THE CORRECT ANSWER IN THE SPACE AT THE RIGHT.*

SAMPLE QUESTION

Column I
Schneider 11/16/75 581932

Column II
A. Schneider 11/16/75 518932
B. Schneider 11/16/75 581932
C. Schnieder 11/16/75 581932
D. Shnieder   11/16/75 518932

The correct answer is B. Only Option B shows the name, date, and number exactly as they are in Column I. Option A has a mistake in the number. Option C has a mistake in the name. Option D has a mistake in the name and in the number. Now answer Questions 1 through 10 in the same manner.

Column I
1. Johnston 12/26/74 659251

Column II
A. Johnson 12/23/74 659251
B. Johston 12/26/74 659251
C. Johnston 12/26/74 695251
D. Johnston 12/26/74 659251

2. Allison 1/26/75 9939256

A. Allison 1/26/75 9939256
B. Alisson 1/26/75 9939256
C. Allison 1/26/76 9399256
D. Allison 1/26/75 9993356

3. Farrell 2/12/75 361251

A. Farell 2/21/75 361251
B. Farrell 2/12/75 361251
C. Farrell 2/21/75 361251
D. Farrell 2/12/75 361151

4. Guerrero 4/28/72 105689
    A. Guererro 4/28/72 105689
    B. Guererro 4/28/72 105986
    C. Guerrero 4/28/72 105869
    D. Guerrero 4/28/72 105689

    4.____

5. McDonnell 6/05/73 478215
    A. McDonnell 6/15/73 478215
    B. McDonnell 6/05/73 478215
    C. McDonnell 6/05/73 472815
    D. MacDonell 6/05/73 478215

    5.____

6. Shepard 3/31/71 075421
    A. Sheperd 3/31/71 075421
    B. Shepard 3/13/71 075421
    C. Shepard 3/31/71 075421
    D. Shepard 3/13/71 075241

    6.____

7. Russell 4/01/69 031429
    A. Russell 4/01/69 031429
    B. Russell 4/10/69 034129
    C. Russell 4/10/69 031429
    D. Russell 4/01/69 034129

    7.____

8. Phillips 10/16/68 961042
    A. Philipps 10/16/68 961042
    B. Phillips 10/16/68 960142
    C. Phillips 10/16/68 961042
    D. Philipps 10/16/68 916042

    8.____

9. Campbell 11/21/72 624856
    A. Campbell 11/21/72 624856
    B. Campbell 11/21/72 624586
    C. Campbell 11/21/72 624686
    D. Campbel 11/21/72 624856

    9.____

10. Patterson 9/18/71 76199176
    A. Patterson 9/18/72 76191976
    B. Patterson 9/18/71 76199176
    C. Patterson 9/18/72 76199176
    D. Patterson 9/18/71 76919176

    10.____

Questions 11-15.

DIRECTIONS: Questions 11 through 15 consist of groups of numbers and letters which you are to compare. For each question, you are to choose the option (A, B,C, or D) in Column I which EXACTLY matches the group of numbers and letters given in Column I.

SAMPLE QUESTION

Column I
B92466

Column II
A. B92644
B. B94266
C. A92466
D. B92466

The correct answer is D. Only Option D in Column II shows the group of numbers and letters EXACTLY as it appears in Column I. Now answer Questions 11 through 15 in the same manner.

<u>Column I</u>

11. 925AC5

<u>Column II</u>
A. 952CA5
B. 925AC5
C. 952AC5
D. 925CA6

11.____

12. Y006925

A. Y060925
B. Y006295
C. Y006529
D. Y006925

12.____

13. J236956

A. J236956
B. J326965
C. J239656
D. J932656

13.____

14. AB6952

A. AB6952
B. AB9625
C. AB9652
D. AB6925

14.____

15. X259361

A. X529361
B. X259631
C. X523961
D. X259361

15.____

Questions 16-25.

DIRECTIONS: Each of questions 16 through 25 consists of three lines of code letters and three lines of numbers. The numbers on each line should correspond with the code letters on the same line in accordance with the table below.

Code Letter	S	V	W	A	Q	M	X	E	G	K
Corresponding Number	0	1	2	3	4	5	5	7	8	9

On some of the lines, an error exists in the coding. Compare the letters and numbers in each question carefully. If you find an error or errors on:
    only one of the lines in the question, mark your answer A;
    any two lines in the question, mark your answer B;
    all three lines in the question, mark your answer C;
    none of the lines in the question, mark your answer D.

4 (#1)

SAMPLE QUESTION

WQGKSXG   2489068
XEKVQMA   6591453
KMAESXV   9527061

In the above sample, the first line is correct since each code letter listed has the correct corresponding number. On the second line, an error exists because code letter E should have the number 7 instead of the number 5. On the third line, an error exists because the code letter A should have the number 3 instead of the number 2. Since there are errors in two of the three lines, the correct answer is B. Now answer Questions 16 through 25 in the same manner.

16. SWQEKGA   0247983   16.____
    KEAVSXM   9731065
    SSAXGKQ   0036894

17. QAMKMVS   4259510   17.____
    MGGEASX   5897306
    KSWMKWS   9125920

18. WKXQWVE   2964217   18.____
    QKXXQVA   4966413
    AWMXGVS   3253810

19. GMMKASE   8559307   19.____
    AWVSKSW   3210902
    QAVSVGK   4310189

20. XGKQSMK   6894049   20.____
    QSVKEAS   4019730
    GSMXKMV   8057951

21. AEKMWSG   3195208   21.____
    MKQSVQK   5940149
    XGQAEVW   6843712

22. XGMKAVS   6858310   22.____
    SKMAWEQ   0953174
    GVMEQSA   8167403

23. VQSKAVE   1489317   23.____
    WQGKAEM   2489375
    MEGKAWQ   5689324

24. XMQVSKG   6541098   24.____
    QMEKEWS   4579720
    KMEVGKG   9571983

25. GKVAMEW   88912572   25.____
    AXMVKAE   3651937
    KWAGMAV   9238531

Questions 26-35.

DIRECTIONS: Each of Questions 26 through 35 consists of a column of figures. For each question, add the column of figures and choose the correct answer from the four choices given.

26.   5,665.43   26.____
      2,356.69
      6,447.24
      7,239.65

      A. 20,698.01   B. 21,709.01
      C. 21,718.01   D. 22,609.01

27.   817,209.55   27.____
      264,354.29
       82,368.76
      849,964.89

      A. 1,893.977.49   B. 1,989,988.39
      C. 2,009,077.39   D. 2,013,897.49

28.   156,366.89   28.____
      249,973.23
      823,229.49
       56,869.45

      A. 1,286,439.06   B. 1,287,521.06
      C. 1,297,539.06   D. 1,296,421.06

29.   23,422.15   29.____
      149,696.24
      238,377.53
       86,289.79
      505,533.63

      A. 989,229.34   B. 999,879.34
      C. 1,003,330.34   D. 1,023,329.34

30. 2,468,926.70
    656,842.28
    49,723.15
    832,369.59

    A. 3,218,062.72 B. 3,808,092.72
    C. 4,007,861.72 D. 4,818,192.72

30.____

31.   524,201.52
    7,775,678.51
    8,345,299.63
    40,628,898.08
    31,374,670.07

    A. 88,646,647.81 B. 88,646,747.91
    C. 88,648,647.91 D. 88,648,747.81

31.____

32. 6,824,829.40
    682,482.94
    5,542,015.27
    775,678.51
    7,732,507.25

    A. 21,557,513.37 B. 21,567,513.37
    C. 22,567,503.37 D. 22,567,513.37

32.____

33. 22,109,405.58
    6,097,093.43
    5,050,073.99
    8,118,050.05
    4,313,980.82

    A. 45,688,593.87 B. 45,688,603.87
    C. 45,689,593.87 D. 45,689,603.87

33.____

34. 79,324,114.19
    99,848,129.74
    43,331,653.31
    41,610,207.14

    A. 264,114,104.38 B. 264,114,114.38
    C. 265,114,114.38 D. 265,214,104.38

34.____

35. 33,729,653.94
    5,959,342.58
  26,052,715.47
    4,452,669.52
    7,079,953.59

A. 76,374,334.10   B. 76,375,334.10
C. 77,274,335.10   D. 77,275,335.10

35._____

Questions 36-40.

DIRECTIONS: Each of Questions 36 through 40 consists of a single number in Column I and four options in Column II. For each question, you are to choose the option (A, B, C, or D) in Column II which EXACTLY matches the number in Column I.

SAMPLE QUESTION

Column I
5965121

Column II
A. 5956121
B. 5965121
C. 5966121
D. 5965211

The correct answer is B. Only Option B shows the number EXACTLY as it appears in Column I. Now answer Questions 36 through 40 in the same manner.

Column I
36. 9643242

Column II
A. 9643242
B. 9462342
C. 9642442
D. 9463242

36._____

37. 3572477

A. 3752477
B. 3725477
C. 3572477
D. 3574277

37._____

38. 5276101

A. 5267101
B. 5726011
C. 5271601
D. 5276101

38._____

39. 4469329

A. 4496329
B. 4469329
C. 4496239
D. 4469239

39._____

40. 2326308

A. 2236308
B. 2233608
C. 2326308
D. 2323608

40._____

KEY (CORRECT ANSWERS)

1.	D	11.	B	21.	A	31.	D
2.	A	12.	D	22.	C	32.	A
3.	B	13.	A	23.	B	33.	B
4.	D	14.	A	24.	D	34.	A
5.	B	15.	D	25.	A	35.	C
6.	C	16.	D	26.	B	36.	A
7.	A	17.	C	27.	D	37.	C
8.	C	18.	A	28.	A	38.	D
9.	A	19.	D	29.	C	39.	B
10.	B	20.	B	30.	C	40.	C

TEST 2

DIRECTIONS: Each question or incomplete statement is followed by several suggested answers or completions. Select the one that BEST answers the question or completes the statement. *PRINT THE LETTER OF THE CORRECT ANSWER IN THE SPACE AT THE RIGHT.*

Questions 1-5.

DIRECTIONS: Each of Questions 1 through 5 consists of a name and a dollar amount. In each question, the name and dollar amount in Column II should be an EXACT copy of the name and dollar amount in Column I. If there is:
    a mistake only in the name, mark your answer A;
    a mistake only in the dollar amount, mark your answer B;
    a mistake in both the name and the dollar amount, mark your answer C;
    no mistake in either the name or the dollar amount, mark your answer D.

SAMPLE QUESTION

Column I
George Peterson
$125.50

Column II
George Petersson
$125.50

Compare the name and dollar amount in Column II with the name and dollar amount in Column I. The name *Petersson* in Column II is spelled *Peterson* in Column I. The amount is the same in both columns. Since there is a mistake only in the name, the answer to the sample question is A. Now answer Questions 1 through 5 in the same manner.

	Column I	Column II	
1.	Susanne Shultz $3440	Susanne Schultz $3440	1.____
2.	Anibal P. Contrucci $2121.61	Anibel P. Contrucci $2112.61	2.____
3.	Eugenio Mendoza $12.45	Eugenio Mendozza $12.45	3.____
4.	Maurice Gluckstadt $4297	Maurice Gluckstadt $4297	4.____
5.	John Pampellonne $4656.94	John Pammpellonne $4566.94	5.____

Questions 6-11.

DIRECTIONS: Each of Questions 6 through 11 consist of a set of names and addresses, which you are to compare. In each question, the name and addresses in Column II should be an EXACT copy of the name and address in Column I. If there is:
    a mistake only in the name, mark your answer A;
    a mistake only in the address, mark your answer B;
    a mistake in both the name and address, mark your answer C;
    no mistake in either the name or address, mark your answer D.

SAMPLE QUESTION

Column I
Michael Filbert
456 Reade Street
New York, N.Y. 10013

Column II
Michael Filbert
645 Reade Street
New York, N.Y. 10013

Since there is a mistake only in the address (the street number should be 456 instead of 645), the answer to the sample question is B. Now answer Questions 6 through 11 in the same manner.

Column I
Column II

6. Hilda Goettelmann
55 Lenox Rd.
Brooklyn, N.Y. 11226

   Hilda Goettelman
55 Lenox Ave.
Brooklyn, N.Y. 11226
   6.____

7. Arthur Sherman
2522 Batchelder St.
Brooklyn, N.Y. 11235

   Arthur Sharman
2522 Batcheder St.
Brooklyn, N.Y. 11253
   7.____

8. Ralph Barnett
300 West 28 Street
New York, New York 10001

   Ralph Barnett
300 West 28 Street
New York, New York 10001
   8.____

9. George Goodwin
135 Palmer Avenue
Staten Island, New York 10302

   George Godwin
135 Palmer Avenue
Staten Island, New York 10302
   9.____

10. Alonso Ramirez
232 West 79 Street
New York, N.Y. 10024

   Alonso Ramirez
223 West 79 Street
New York, N.Y. 10024
   10.____

11. Cynthia Graham
149-34 83 Street
Howard Beach, N.Y. 11414

   Cynthia Graham
149-35 83 Street
Howard Beach, N.Y. 11414
   11.____

Questions 12-20.

DIRECTIONS: Questions 12 through 20 are problems in subtraction. For each question do the subtraction and select your answer from the four choices given.

12. 232,921.85
    -179,587.68

    A. 52,433.17   B. 52,434.17
    C. 53,334.17   D. 53,343,17

    12.____

13. 5,531,876.29
    -3,897,158.36

    A. 1,634,717.93   B. 1,644,718.93
    C. 1,734,717.93   D. 1,7234,718.93

    13.____

14. 1,482,658.22
    -937,925.76

    A. 544,633.46   B. 544,732.46
    C. 545,632.46   D. 545,732.46

    14.____

15. 937,828.17
    -259,673.88

    A. 678,154.29   B. 679,154.29
    C. 688,155.39   D. 699,155.39

    15.____

16. 760,412.38
    -263,465.95

    A. 496,046.43   B. 496,946.43
    C. 496,956.43   D. 497,046.43

    16.____

17. 3,203,902.26
    -2,933,087.96

    A. 260,814.30   B. 269,824.30
    C. 270,814.30   D. 270,824.30

    17.____

18. 1,023,468.71
    -934,678.88

    A. 88,780.83   B. 88,789.83
    C. 88,880.83   D. 88,889.83

    18.____

19. 831,549.47
    -772,814.78

    A. 58,734.69   B. 58,834.69
    C. 59,735.69   D. 59,834.69

20. 6,306,181.74
    -3,617,376.99

    A. 2,687,904.99   B. 2,688,904.99
    C. 2,689,804.99   D. 2,799,905.99

Questions 21-30.

DIRECTIONS: Each of Questions 21 through 30 consists of three lines of code letters and three lines of numbers. The numbers on each line should correspond with the code letters on the same line in accordance with the table below.

Code Letter	J	U	B	T	Y	D	K	R	L	P
Corresponding Number	0	1	2	3	4	5	5	7	8	9

On some of the lines, an error exists in the coding. Compare the letters and numbers in each question carefully. If you find an error or errors on:
  only *one* of the lines in the question, mark your answer A;
  any *two* lines in the question, mark your answer B;
  all *three* lines in the question, mark your answer C;
  none of the lines in the question, mark your answer D.

SAMPLE QUESTION

BJRPYUR   2079417
DTBPYKJ   5328460
YKLDBLT   4685283

In the above sample, the first line is correct since each code letter listed has the correct corresponding number. On the second line, an error exists because code letter P should have the number 9 instead of the number 8. The third line is correct since each code letter listed has the correct corresponding number. Since there is an error in *one* of the three lines, the correct answer is A. Now answer Questions 21 through 30 in the same manner.

21. BYPDTJL   2495308
    PLRDTJU   9815301
    DTJRYLK   5207486

22. RPBYRJK   7934706
    PKTYLBU   9624821
    KDLPJYR   6489047

23.	TPYBUJR	3942107	23.____
	BYRKPTU	2476931	
	DUKPYDL	5169458	
24.	KBYDLPL	6345898	24.____
	BLRKBRU	2876261	
	JTULDYB	0318542	
25.	LDPYDKR	8594567	25.____
	BDKDRJL	2565708	
	BDRPLUJ	2679810	
26.	PLRLBPU	9858291	26.____
	LPYKRDJ	88936750	
	TDKPDTR	3569527	
27.	RKURPBY	7617924	27.____
	RYUKPTJ	7426930	
	RTKPTJD	7369305	
28.	DYKPBJT	5469203	28.____
	KLPJBTL	6890238	
	TKPLBJP	3698209	
29.	BTPRJYL	2397148	29.____
	LDKUTYR	8561347	
	YDBLRPJ	4528190	
30.	ULPBKYT	1892643	30.____
	KPDTRBJ	6953720	
	YLKJPTB	4860932	

KEY (CORRECT ANSWERS)

1.	A	11.	D	21.	B
2.	C	12.	C	22.	C
3.	A	13.	A	23.	D
4.	D	14.	B	24.	B
5.	C	15.	A	25.	A
6.	C	16.	B	26.	C
7.	C	17.	C	27.	A
8.	D	18.	B	28.	D
9.	A	19.	A	29.	B
10.	B	20.	B	30.	D

CLERICAL ABILITIES
EXAMINATION SECTION
TEST 1

DIRECTIONS: Each question or incomplete statement is followed by several suggested answers or completions. Select the one that BEST answers the question or completes the statement. *PRINT THE LETTER OF THE CORRECT ANSWER IN THE SPACE AT THE RIGHT.*

Questions 1-4.

DIRECTIONS: Questions 1 through 4 are to be answered on the basis of the information given below.

The most commonly used filing system and the one that is easiest to learn is alphabetical filing. This involves putting records in an A to Z order, according to the letters of the alphabet. The name of a person is filed by using the following order: first, the surname or last name; second, the first name; third, the middle name or middle initial. For example, *Henry C. Young* is filed under *Y* and thereafter under *Young, Henry C.* The name of a company is filed in the same way. For example, *Long Cabinet Co.* is filed under *L* while *John T. Long Cabinet Co.* is filed under *L* and thereafter under *Long, John T. Cabinet Co.*

1. The one of the following which lists the names of persons in the CORRECT alphabetical order is:
   A. Mary Carrie, Helen Carrol, James Carson, John Carter
   B. James Carson, Mary Carrie, John Carter, Helen Carrol
   C. Helen Carrol, James Carson, John Carter, Mary Carrie
   D. John Carter, Helen Carrol, Mary Carrie, James Carson

1.____

2. The one of the following which lists the names of persons in the CORRECT alphabetical order is:
   A. Jones, John C.; Jones, John A.; Jones, John P.; Jones, John K.
   B. Jones, John P.; Jones, John K.; Jones, John C.; Jones, John A.
   C. Jones, John A.; Jones, John C.; Jones, John K.; Jones, John P.
   D. Jones, John K.; Jones, John C.; Jones, John A.; Jones, John P.

2.____

3. The one of the following which lists the names of the companies in the CORRECT alphabetical order is:
   A. Blane Co., Blake Co., Block Co., Blear Co.
   B. Blake Co., Blane Co., Blear Co., Block Co.
   C. Block Co., Blear Co., Blane Co., Blake Co.
   D. Blear Co., Blake Co., Blane Co., Block Co.

3.____

4. You are to return to the file an index card on *Barry C. Wayne Materials and Supplies Co.*
Of the following, the CORRECT alphabetical group that you should return the index card to is
A. A to G   B. H to M   C. N to S   D. T to Z

Questions 5-10.

DIRECTIONS: In each of Questions 5 through 10, the names of four people are given. For each question, choose as your answer the one of the four names given which should be filed FIRST according to the usual system of alphabetical filing of names, as described in the following paragraph.

In filing names, you must start with the last name. Names are filed in order of the first letter of the last name, then the second letter, etc. Therefore, BAILY would be filed before BROWN, which would be filed before COLT. A name with fewer letters of the same type comes first, i.e., Smith before Smithe. If the last names are the same, the names are filed alphabetically by the first name. If the first name is an initial, a name with an initial would come before a first name that starts with the same letter as the initial. Therefore, I. BROWN would come before IRA BROWN. Finally, if both last name and first name are the same, the name would be filed alphabetically by the middle name, once again an initial coming before a middle name which starts with the same letter as the initial. If there is no middle name at all, the name would come before those with middle initials or names.

SAMPLE QUESTION: A. Lester Daniels
                                  B. William Dancer
                                  C. Nathan Danzig
                                  D. Dan Lester

The last names beginning with D are filed before the last name beginning with L. Since DANIELS, DANCER, and DANZIG all begin with the same three letters, you must look at the fourth letter of the last name to determine which name should be filed first. C comes before I or Z in the alphabet, so DANCER is filed before DANIELS or DANZIG. Therefore, the answer to the above sample question is B.

5. A. Scott Biala
   B. Mary Byala
   C. Martin Baylor
   D. Francis Bauer

6. A. Howard J. Black
   B. Howard Black
   C. J. Howard Black
   D. John H. Black

7. A. Theodora Garth Kingston
   B. Theadore Barth Kingston
   C. Thomas Kingston
   D. Thomas T. Kingston

8. A. Paulette Mary Huerta
    B. Paul M. Huerta
    C. Paulette L. Huerta
    D. Peter A. Huerta

9. A. Martha Hunt Morgan
    B. Martin Hunt Morgan
    C. Mary H. Morgan
    D. Martine H. Morgan

10. A. James T. Meerschaum
    B. James M. Mershum
    C. James F. Mearshaum
    D. James N. Meshum

Questions 11-14.

DIRECTIONS: Questions 11 through 14 are to be answered SOLELY on the basis of the following information.

You are required to file various documents in file drawers which are labeled according to the following pattern:

DOCUMENTS

MEMOS		LETTERS	
File	Subject	File	Subject
84PM1	(A-L)	84PC1	(A-L)
84PM2	(M-Z)	84PC2	(M-Z)

REPORTS		INQUIRIES	
File	Subject	File	Subject
84PR1	(A-L)	84PQ1	(A-L)
84PR2	(M-Z)	84PQ2	(M-Z)

11. A letter dealing with a burglary should be filed in the drawer labeled
    A. 84PM1   B. 84PC1   C. 84PR1   D. 84PQ2

12. A report on Statistics should be found in the drawer labeled
    A. 84PM1   B. 84PC2   C. 84PR2   D. 84PQS

13. An inquiry is received about parade permit procedures. It should be filed in the drawer labeled
    A. 84PM2   B. 84PC1   C. 84PR1   D. 84PQ2

14. A police officer has a question about a robbery report you filed. You should pull this file from the drawer labeled
    A. 84PM1   B. 84PM2   C. 84PR1   D. 84PR2

Questions 15-22.

DIRECTIONS: Each of Questions 15 through 22 consists of four or six numbered names. For each question, choose the option (A, B, C, or D) which indicates the order in which the names should be filed in accordance with the following filing instructions:
- File alphabetically according to last name, then first name, then middle initial.
- File according to each successive letter within a name.
- When comparing two names in which the letters in the longer name are identical to the corresponding letters in the shorter name, the shorter name is filed first.
- When the last names are the same, initials are always filed before names beginning with the same letter.

15. I.   Ralph Robinson
     II. Alfred Ross
     III. Luis Robles
     IV. James Roberts

The CORRECT filing sequence for the above names should be
A. IV, II, I, III B. I, IV, III, II C. III, IV, I, II D. IV, I, III, II

16. I.   Irwin Goodwin
     II. Inez Gonzalez
     III. Irene Goodman
     IV. Ira S. Goodwin
     V.   Ruth I. Goldstein
     VI. M.B. Goodman

The CORRECT filing sequence for the above names should be
A. V, II, I, IV, III, VI   B. V, II, VI, III, IV, I
C. V, II, III, VI, IV, I   D. V, II, III, VI, I, IV

17. I.   George Allan
     II. Gregory Allen
     III. Gary Allen
     IV. George Allen

The CORRECT filing sequence for the above names should be
A. IV, III, I, II B. I, IV, II, III C. III, IV, I, II D. I, III, IV, II

5 (#1)

18. I. Simon Kauffman
     II. Leo Kaufman
     III. Robert Kaufmann
     IV. Paul Kauffmann

    The CORRECT filing sequence for the above names should be
    A. I, IV, II, III   B. II, IV, III, I   C. III, II, IV, I   D. I, II, III, IV

18.____

19. I. Roberta Williams
     II. Robin Wilson
     III. Roberta Wilson
     IV. Robin Williams

    The CORRECT filing sequence for the above names should be
    A. III, II, IV, I   B. I, IV, III, II   C. I, II, III, IV   D. III, I, II, IV

19.____

20. I. Lawrence Shultz
     II. Albert Schultz
     III. Theodore Schwartz
     IV. Thomas Schwarz
     V. Alvin Schultz
     VI. Leonard Shultz

    The CORRECT filing sequence for the above names should be
    A. II, V, III, IV, I, VI   B. IV, III, V, I, II, VI
    C. II, V, I, VI, III, IV   D. I, VI, II, V, III, IV

20.____

21. I. McArdle
     II. Mayer
     III. Maletz
     IV. McNiff
     V. Meyer
     VI. MacMahon

    The CORRECT filing sequence for the above names should be
    A. I, IV, VI, III, II, V   B. II, I, IV, VI, III, V
    C. VI, III, II, I, IV, V   D. VI, III, II, V, I, IV

21.____

22. I. Jack E. Johnson
     II. R.H. Jackson
     III. Bertha Jackson
     IV. J.T. Johnson
     V. Ann Johns
     VI. John Jacobs

    The CORRECT filing sequence for the above names should be
    A. II, III, VI, V, IV, I   B. III, II, VI, V, IV, I
    C. VI, II, III, I, V, IV   D. III, II, VI, IV, V, I

22.____

Questions 23-30.

DIRECTIONS: The code table below shows 10 letters with matching numbers. For each question, there are three sets of letters. Each set of letters is followed by a set of numbers which may or may not match their correct letter according to the code table. For each question, check all three sets of letters and numbers and mark your answer:
- A. if no pairs are correctly matched
- B. if only one pair is correctly matched
- C. if only two pairs are correctly matched
- D. if all three pairs are correctly matched

CODE TABLE

T	M	V	D	S	P	R	G	B	H
1	2	3	4	5	6	7	8	9	0

SAMPLE QUESTION: TMVDSP – 123456
RGBHTM – 789011
DSPRGB – 256789

In the sample question above, the first set of numbers correctly match its set of letters. But the second and third pairs contain mistakes. In the second pair, M is correctly matched with number 1. According to the code table, letter M should be correctly matched with number 2. In the third pair, the letter D is incorrectly matched with number 2. According to the code table, letter D should be correctly matched with number 4. Since only one of the pairs is correctly matched, the answer to this sample question is B.

23. RSBMRM – 759262
    GDSRVH – 845730
    VDBRTM - 349713

24. TGVSDR – 183247
    SMHRDP – 520647
    TRMHSR - 172057

25. DSPRGM – 456782
    MVDBHT – 234902
    HPMDBT – 062491

26. BVPTRD – 936184
    GDPHMB – 807029
    GMRHMV - 827032

27. MGVRSH – 283750
    TRDMBS – 174295
    SPRMGV - 567283

23.____

24.____

25.____

26.____

27.____

28. SGBSDM – 489542
    MGHPTM – 290612
    MPBMHT - 269301

29. TDPBHM – 146902
    VPBMRS – 369275
    GDMBHM - 842902

30. MVPTBV – 236194
    PDRTMB – 47128
    BGTMSM - 981232

28.____

29.____

30.____

KEY (CORRECT ANSWERS)

1.	A	11.	B	21.	C
2.	C	12.	C	22.	B
3.	B	13.	D	23.	B
4.	D	14.	D	24.	B
5.	D	15.	D	25.	C
6.	B	16.	C	26.	A
7.	B	17.	D	27.	D
8.	B	18.	A	28.	A
9.	A	19.	B	29.	D
10.	C	20.	A	30.	A

TEST 2

DIRECTIONS: Each question or incomplete statement is followed by several suggested answers or completions. Select the one that BEST answers the question or completes the statement. *PRINT THE LETTER OF THE CORRECT ANSWER IN THE SPACE AT THE RIGHT.*

Questions 1-10.

DIRECTIONS: Questions 1 through 10 each consists of two columns, each containing four lines of names, numbers and/or addresses. For each question, compare the lines in Column I with the lines in Column II to see if they match exactly, and mark your answer A, B, C, or D, according to the following instructions:
    A. all four lines match exactly
    B. only three lines match exactly
    C. only two lines match exactly
    D. only one line matches exactly

<u>COLUMN I</u>   <u>COLUMN II</u>

1.   I.   Earl Hodgson   Earl Hodgson   1.____
     II.   1409870   1408970
     III.   Shore Ave.   Schore Ave.
     IV.   Macon Rd.   Macon Rd.

2.   I.   9671485   9671485   2.____
     II.   470 Astor Court   470 Astor Court
     III.   Halprin, Phillip   Halperin, Phillip
     IV.   Frank D. Poliseo   Frank D. Poliseo

3.   I.   Tandem Associates   Tandom Associates   3.____
     II.   144-17 Northern Blvd.   144-17 Northern Blvd.
     III.   Alberta Forchi   Albert Forchi
     IV.   Kings Park, NY 10751   Kings Point, NY 10751

4.   I.   Bertha C. McCormack   Bertha C. McCormack   4.____
     II.   Clayton, MO   Clayton, MO
     III.   976-4242   976-4242
     IV.   New City, NY 10951   New City, NY 10951

5.   I.   George C. Morill   George C. Morrill   5.____
     II.   Columbia, SC 29201   Columbia, SD 29201
     III.   Louis Ingham   Louis Ingham
     IV.   3406 Forest Ave.   3406 Forest Ave.

6.   I.   506 S. Elliott Pl.   506 S. Elliott Pl.   6.____
     II.   Herbert Hall   Hurbert Hall
     III.   4712 Rockaway Pkway   4712 Rockaway Pkway
     IV.   169 E. 7 St.   169 E. 7 St.

7. I.   345 Park Ave.   345 Park Pl.   7.____
    II. Colman Oven Corp.   Coleman Oven Corp.
    III. Robert Conte   Robert Conti
    IV. 6179846   6179846

8. I.   Grigori Schierber   Grigori Schierber   8.____
    II. Des Moines, Iowa   Des Moines, Iowa
    III. Gouverneur Hospital   Gouverneur Hospital
    IV. 91-35 Cresskill Pl.   91-35 Cresskill Pl.

9. I.   Jeffery Janssen   Jeffrey Janssen   9.____
    II. 8041071   8041071
    III. 40 Rockefeller Plaza   40 Rockafeller Plaza
    IV. 407 6 St.   406 7 St.

10. I.   5971996   5871996   10.____
    II. 3113 Knickerbocker Ave.   31123 Knickerbocker Ave.
    III. 8434 Boston Post Rd.   8424 Boston Post Rd.
    IV. Penn Station   Penn Station

Questions 11-14.

DIRECTIONS: Questions 11 through 14 are to be answered by looking at the four groups of names and addresses listed below (I, II, III, and IV), and then finding out the number of groups that have their corresponding numbered lies exactly the same.

	GROUP I	GROUP II
Line 1.	Richmond General Hospital	Richman General Hospital
Line 2.	Geriatric Clinic	Geriatric Clinic
Line 3.	3975 Paerdegat St.	3975 Peardegat St.
Line 4.	Loudonville, New York 11538	Londonville, New York 11538

	GROUP III	GROUP IV
Line 1.	Richmond General Hospital	Richmend General Hospital
Line 2.	Geriatric Clinic	Geriatric Clinic
Line 3.	3795 Paerdegat St.	3975 Paerdegat St.
Line 4.	Loudonville, New York 11358	Loudonville, New York 11538

1. In how many groups is line one exactly the same?   11.____
    A. Two   B. Three   C. Four   D. None

12. In how many groups is line two exactly the same?   12.____
    A. Two   B. Three   C. Four   D. None

13. In how many groups is line three exactly the same?   13.____
    A. Two   B. Three   C. Four   D. None

3 (#2)

14. In how many groups is line four exactly the same? 14.____
 A. Two B. Three C. Four D. None

Questions 15-18.

DIRECTIONS: Each of Questions 15 through 18 has two lists of names and addresses. Each list contains three sets of names and addresses. Check each of the three sets in the list on the right to see if they are the same as the corresponding set in the list on the left. Mark your answers:
 A. if none of the sets in the right list are the same as those in the left list
 B. if only one of the sets in the right list is the same as those in the left list
 C. if only two of the sets in the right list are the same as those in the left list
 D. if all three sets in the right list are the same as those in the left list

15. Mary T. Berlinger Mary T. Berlinger 15.____
 2351 Hampton St. 2351 Hampton St.
 Monsey, N.Y. 20117 Monsey, N.Y. 20117

 Eduardo Benes Eduardo Benes
 483 Kingston Avenue 473 Kingston Avenue
 Central Islip, N.Y. 11734 Central Islip, N.Y. 11734

 Alan Carrington Fuchs Alan Carrington Fuchs
 17 Gnarled Hollow Road 17 Gnarled Hollow Road
 Los Angeles, CA 91635 Los Angeles, CA 91685

16. David John Jacobson David John Jacobson 16.____
 178 34 St. Apt. 4C 178 53 St. Apt. 4C
 New York, N.Y. 00927 New York, N.Y. 00927

 Ann-Marie Calonella Ann-Marie Calonella
 7243 South Ridge Blvd. 7243 South Ridge Blvd.
 Bakersfield, CA 96714 Bakersfield, CA 96714

 Pauline M. Thompson Pauline M. Thomson
 872 Linden Ave. 872 Linden Ave.
 Houston, Texas 70321 Houston, Texas 70321

17. Chester LeRoy Masterton Chester LeRoy Masterson 17.____
 152 Lacy Rd. 152 Lacy Rd.
 Kankakee, Ill. 54532 Kankakee, Ill. 54532

 William Maloney William Maloney
 S. LaCrosse Pla. S. LaCross Pla.
 Wausau, Wisconsin 52136 Wausau, Wisconsin 52146

 Cynthia V. Barnes Cynthia V. Barnes
 16 Pines Rd. 16 Pines Rd.
 Greenpoint, Miss. 20376 Greenpoint,, Miss. 20376

4 (#2)

18. Marcel Jean Frontenac
    8 Burton On The Water
    Calender, Me. 01471

    J. Scott Marsden
    174 S. Tipton St.
    Cleveland, Ohio

    Lawrence T. Haney
    171 McDonough St.
    Decatur, Ga. 31304

    Marcel Jean Frontenac
    6 Burton On The Water
    Calender, Me. 01471

    J. Scott Marsden
    174 Tipton St.
    Cleveland, Ohio

    Lawrence T. Haney
    171 McDonough St.
    Decatur, Ga. 31304

18.____

Questions 19-26.

DIRECTIONS: Each of Questions 19 through 26 has two lists of numbers. Each list contains three sets of numbers. Check each of the three sets in the list on the right to see if they are the same as the corresponding set in the list on the left. Mark your answers:
- A. if none of the sets in the right list are the same as those in the left list
- B. if only one of the sets in the right list is the same as those in the left list
- C. if only two of the sets in the right list are the same as those in the left list
- D. if all three sets in the right list are the same as those in the left lists

19. 7354183476
    4474747744
    5791430231

    7354983476
    4474747774
    57914302311

19.____

20. 7143592185
    8344517699
    9178531263

    7143892185
    8344518699
    9178531263

20.____

21. 2572114731
    8806835476
    8255831246

    257214731
    8806835476
    8255831246

21.____

22. 331476853821
    6976658532996
    3766042113715

    331476858621
    6976655832996
    3766042113745

22.____

23. 8806663315
    74477138449
    211756663666

    88066633115
    74477138449
    211756663666

23.____

24. 990006966996   99000696996   24._____
    53022219743   53022219843
    4171171117717   4171171177717

25. 24400222433004   24400222433004   25._____
    5300030055000355   5300030055500355
    20000075532002022   20000075532002022

26. 611166640660001116   61116664066001116   26._____
    7111300117001100733   7111300117001100733
    26666446664476518   26666446664476518

Questions 27-30.

DIRECTIONS: Questions 27 through 30 are to be answered by picking the answer which is in the correct numerical order, from the lowest number to the highest number, in each question.

27. A. 44533, 44518, 44516, 44547   27._____
    B. 44516, 44518, 44533, 44547
    C. 44547, 44533, 44518, 44516
    D. 44518, 44516, 44547, 44533

28. A. 95587, 95593, 95601, 95620   28._____
    B. 95601, 95620, 95587, 95593
    C. 95593, 95587, 95601. 95620
    D. 95620, 95601, 95593, 95587

29. A. 232212, 232208, 232232, 232223   29._____
    B. 232208, 232223, 232212, 232232
    C. 232208, 232212, 232223, 232232
    D. 232223, 232232, 232208, 232208

30. A. 113419, 113521, 113462, 113462   30._____
    B. 113588, 113462, 113521, 113419
    C. 113521, 113588, 113419, 113462
    D. 113419, 113462, 113521, 113588

KEY (CORRECT ANSWERS)

1.	C	11.	A	21.	C
2.	B	12.	C	22.	A
3.	D	13.	A	23.	D
4.	A	14.	A	24.	A
5.	C	15.	C	25.	C
6.	B	16.	B	26.	C
7.	D	17.	B	27.	B
8.	A	18.	B	28.	A
9.	D	19.	B	29.	C
10.	C	20.	B	30.	D

RECORD KEEPING
EXAMINATION SECTION
TEST 1

DIRECTIONS: Each question or incomplete statement is followed by several suggested answers or completions. Select the one that BEST answers the question or completes the statement. *PRINT THE LETTER OF THE CORRECT ANSWER IN THE SPACE AT THE RIGHT.*

Questions 1-15.

DIRECTIONS: Questions 1 through 15 are to be answered on the basis of the following list of company names below. Arrange a file alphabetically, word-by-word, disregarding punctuation, conjunctions, and apostrophes. Then answer the questions.

    A Bee C Reading Materials
    ABCO Parts
    A Better Course for Test Preparation
    AAA Auto Parts Co.
    A-Z Auto Parts, Inc.
    Aabar Books
    Abbey, Joanne
    Boman-Sylvan Law Firm
    BMW Autowerks
    C Q Service Company
    Chappell-Murray, Inc.
    E&E Life Insurance
    Emcrisco
    Gigi Arts
    Gordon, Jon & Associates
    SOS Plumbing
    Schmidt, J.B. Co.

1. Which of these files should appear FIRST?
   A. ABCO Parts
   B. A Bee C Reading Materials
   C. A Better Course for Test Preparation
   D. AAA Auto Parts Co.

   1.____

2. Which of these files should appear SECOND?
   A. A-Z Auto Parts, Inc.
   B. A Bee C Reading Materials
   C. A Better Course for Test Preparation
   D. AAA Auto Parts Co.

   2.____

2 (#1)

3. Which of these files should appear THIRD?   3.____
    A. ABCO Parts   B. A Bee C Reading Materials
    C. Aabar Books   D. AAA Auto Parts Co.

4. Which of these files should appear FOURTH?   4.____
    A. Aabar Books   B. ABCO Parts
    C. Abbey, Joanne   D. AAA Auto Parts Co.

5. Which of these files should appear LAST?   5.____
    A. Gordon, Jon & Associates   B. Gigi Arts
    C. Schmidt, J.B. Co.   D. SOS Plumbing

6. Which of these files should appear between A-Z Auto Parts, Inc. and Abbey,   6.____
   Joanne?
    A. A Bee C Reading Materials
    B. AAA Auto Parts Co.
    C. ABCO Parts
    D. A Better Course for Test Preparation

7. Which of these files should appear between ABCO Parts and Aabar Books?   7.____
    A. A Bee C Reading Materials   B. Abbey, Joanne
    C. Aabar Books   D. A-Z Auto Parts

8. Which of these files should appear between Abbey, Joanne and Boman-Sylvan   8.____
   Law Firm?
    A. A Better Course for Test Preparation
    B. BMW Autowerks
    C. Chappell-Murray, Inc.
    D. Aabar Books

9. Which of these files should appear between Abbey, Joanne and C Q Service?   9.____
    A. A-Z Auto Parts, Inc.   B. BMW Autowerks
    C. Choices A and B   D. Chappell-Murray, Inc.

10. Which of these files should appear between C Q Service Company and   10.____
    Emcrisco?
    A. Chappell-Murray, Inc.   B. E&E Life Insurance
    C. Gigi Arts   D. Choices A and B

11. Which of these files should NOT appear between C Q Service Company and   11.____
    E&E Life Insurance?
    A. Gordon, Jon & Associates   B. Emcrisco
    C. Gigi Arts   D. All of the above

12. Which of these files should appear between Chappell-Murray, Inc. and Gigi Arts? 12.____
    A. C Q Service Inc., E&E Life Insurance, and Emcrisco
    B. Emcrisco, E&E Life Insurance, and Gordon, Jon & Associates
    C. E&E Life Insurance, and Emcrisco
    D. Emcrisco and Gordon, Jon & Associates

13. Which of these files should appear between Gordon, Jon & Associates and SOS Plumbing? 13.____
    A. Gigi Arts
    B. Schmidt, J.B. Co.
    C. Choices A and B
    D. None of the above

14. Each of the choices lists the four files in their proper alphabetical order EXCEPT 14.____
    A. E&E Life Insurance; Gigi Arts; Gordon, Jon & Associates; SOS Plumbing
    B. E&E Life Insurance; Emcrisco; Gigi Arts; SOS Plumbing
    C. Emcrisco; Gordon, Jon & Associates; SOS Plumbing; Schmidt, J.B. Co.
    D. Emcrisco; Gigi Arts; Gordon, Jon & Associates; SOS Plumbing

15. Which of the choices lists the four files in their proper alphabetical order? 15.____
    A. Gigi Arts; Gordon, Jon & Associates; SOS Plumbing; Schmidt, J.B. Co.
    B. Gordon, Jon & Associates; Gigi Arts; Schmidt, J.B. Co.; SOS Plumbing
    C. Gordon, Jon & Associates; Gigi Arts; SOS Plumbing; Schmidt, J.B. Co.
    D. Gigi Arts; Gordon, Jon & Associates; Schmidt, J.B. Co.; SOS Plumbing

16. The alphabetical filing order of two businesses with identical names is determined by the 16.____
    A. length of time each business has been operating
    B. addresses of the businesses
    C. last name of the company president
    D. no one of the above

17. In an alphabetical filing system, if a business name includes a number, it should be 17.____
    A. disregarded
    B. considered a number and placed at the end of an alphabetical section
    C. treated as though it were written in words and alphabetized accordingly
    D. considered a number and placed at the beginning of an alphabetical section

18. If a business name includes a contraction (such as *don't* or *it's*), how should that word be treated in an alphabetical system? 18.____
    A. Divide the word into its separate parts and treat it as two words
    B. Ignore the letters that come after the apostrophe
    C. Ignore the word that contains the contraction
    D. Ignore the apostrophe and consider all letters in the contraction

19. In what order should the parts of an address be considered when using an alphabetical filing system?   19._____
    A. City or town; state; street name; house or building number
    B. State; city or town; street name; house or building number
    C. House or building number; street name; city or town; state
    D. Street name; city or town; state

20. A business record should be cross-referenced when a(n)   20._____
    A. organization is known by an abbreviated name
    B. business has a name change because of a sale, incorporation, or other reason
    C. business is known by a *coined* or common name which differs from a dictionary spelling
    D. all of the above

21. A geographical filing system is MOST effective when   21._____
    A. location is more important than name
    B. many names or titles sound alike
    C. dealing with companies who have offices all over the world
    D. filing personal and business files

Questions 22-25.

DIRECTIONS: Questions 22 through 25 are to be answered on the basis of the list of items below, which are to be filed geographically. Organize the items geographically and then answer the questions.

    I. University Press at Berkeley, U.S.
    II. Maria Sanchez, Mexico City, Mexico
    III. Great Expectations Ltd. in London, England
    IV. Justice League, Cape Town, South Africa, Africa
    V. Crown Pearls Ltd. in London, England
    VI. Joseph Prasad in London, England

22. Which of the following arrangements of the items is composed according to the policy of: *Continent, Country, City, Firm or Individual Name*?   22._____
    A. V, III, IV, VI, II, I
    B. IV, V, III, VI, II, I
    C. I, IV, V, III, VI, II
    D. IV, V, III, VI, I, II

23. Which of the following files is arranged according to the policy of: *Continent, Country, City, Firm or Individual Name*?   23._____
    A. South Africa; Africa; Cape Town; Justice League
    B. Mexico; Mexico City; Maria Sanchez
    C. North America; United States; Berkeley; University Press
    D. England; Europe; London; Prasad, Joseph

24. Which of the following arrangements of the items is composed according to the policy of: *Country, City, Firm or Individual Name*? 24.____
    A. V, VI, III, II, IV, I
    B. I, V, VI, III, II, IV
    C. VI, V, III, II, IV, I
    D. V, III, VI, II, IV, I

25. Which of the following files is arranged according to a policy of: *Country, City, Firm or Individual Name*? 25.____
    A. England; London; Crown Pearls Ltd.
    B. North America; United States; Berkeley; University Press
    C. Africa; Cape Town; Justice League
    D. Mexico City; Mexico; Maria Sanchez

26. Under which of the following circumstances would a phonetic filing system be MOST effective? 26.____
    A. When the person in charge of filing can't spell very well
    B. With large files with names that sound alike
    C. With large files with names that are spelled alike
    D. All of the above

Questions 27-29.

DIRECTIONS: Questions 27 through 29 are to be answered on the basis of the following list of numerical files.

    I.   391-023-100
    II.   361-132-170
    III. 385-732-200
    IV.   381-432-150
    V.   391-632-387
    VI.   361-423-303
    VII. 391-123-271

27. Which of the following arrangements of the files follows a consecutive-digit system? 27.____
    A. II, III, IV, I   B. I, V, VII, III   C. II, IV, III, I   D. III, I, V, VII

28. Which of the following arrangements follows a terminal-digit system? 28.____
    A. I, VII, II, IV, III
    B. II, I, IV, V, VII
    C. VII, VI, V, IV, III
    D. I, IV, II, III, VII

29. Which of the following lists follows a middle-digit system? 29.____
    A. I, VII, II, VI, IV, V, III
    B. I, II, VII, IV, VI, V, III
    C. VII, II, I, III, V, VI, IV
    D. VII, I, II, IV, VI, V, III

Questions 30-31.

DIRECTIONS: Questions 30 and 31 are to be answered on the basis of the following information.

   I. Reconfirm Laura Bates appointment with James Caldecort on December 12 at 9:30 A.M.
   II. Laurence Kinder contact Julia Lucas on August 3 and set up a meeting for week of September 23 at 4 P.M.
   III. John Lutz contact Larry Waverly on August 3 and set up appointment for September 23 at 9:30 A.M.
   IV. Call for tickets for Gerry Stanton August 21 for New Jersey on September 23, flight 143 at 4:43 P.M.

30. A chronological file for the above information would be
    A. IV, III, II, I   B. III, II, IV, I   C. IV, II, III, I   D. III, I, II, IV

31. Using the above information, a chronological file for the date September 23 would be
    A. II, III, IV   B. III, I, IV   C. III, II, IV   D. IV, III, II

Questions 32-34.

DIRECTIONS: Questions 32 through 34 are to be answered on the basis of the following information.

   I. Call Roger Epstein, Ashoke Naipaul, Jon Anderson, and Sara Washingon on April 19 at 1:00 P.M. to set up meeting with Alika D'Ornay for June 6 in New York.
   II. Call Martin Ames before noon on April 19 to confirm afternoon meeting with Bob Greenwood on April 20th.
   III. Set up meeting room at noon for 2:30 P.M. meeting on April 19th.
   IV. Ashley Stanton contact Bob Greenwood at 9:00 A.M. on April 20 and set up meeting for June 6 at 8:30 A.M.
   V. Carol Guiland contact Shelby Van Ness during afternoon of April 20 and set up meeting for June 6 at 10:00 A.M.
   VI. Call airline and reserve tickets on June 6 for Roger Epstein trip to Denver on July 8.
   VII. Meeting at 2:30 P.M. on April 19th.

32. A chronological file for all of the above information would be
    A. II, I, III, VII, V, IV, VI   B. III, VII, II, I, IV, V, VI
    C. III, VII, I, II, V, IV, VI   D. II, III, I, VII, IV, V, VI

33. A chronological file for the date of April 19th would be
    A. II, III, VII, I   B. II, III, I, VII   C. VII, I, III, II   D. III, VII, I, II

34. Add the following information to the file, and then create a chronological file for April 20th: VIII. April 20: 3:00 P.M. meeting between Bob Greenwood and Martin Ames.
    A. IV, V, VIII   B. IV, VIII, V   C. VIII, V, IV   D. V, IV, VIII

35. The PRIMARY advantage of computer records over a manual system is
    A. speed of retrieval
    B. accuracy
    C. cost
    D. potential file loss

KEY (CORRECT ANSWERS)

1.	B	11.	D	21.	A	31.	C
2.	C	12.	C	22.	B	32.	D
3.	D	13.	B	23.	C	33.	B
4.	A	14.	C	24.	D	34.	A
5.	D	15.	D	25.	A	35.	A
6.	C	16.	B	26.	B		
7.	B	17.	C	27.	C		
8.	B	18.	D	28.	D		
9.	C	19.	A	29.	A		
10.	D	20.	D	30.	B		

EXAMINATION SECTION
TEST 1

DIRECTIONS: Each question or incomplete statement is followed by several suggested answers or completions. Select the one that BEST answers the question or completes the statement. *PRINT THE LETTER OF THE CORRECT ANSWER IN THE SPACE AT THE RIGHT.*

Questions 1-5.

DIRECTIONS: Questions 1 through 5 are to be answered on the basis of the following fact pattern.

Astrid's son, Carlos, attends the local high school. Carlos and another student, Manny, have been bullying another student both on and off school premises. The high school principal has notified the New York Police Department School Safety Unit of the issue. The principal has also been in touch with Astrid and Manny's mother, Mary. Mary believes Carlos is a bad influence to her son, Manny. After obtaining Astrid's phone number, Mary called Astrid and made threats towards her and Carlos. She indicated that if Carlos did not stay away from her son, Manny, she would have them both killed. The next day after school, Carlos is jumped by a group of teenagers and his leg is broken in the brawl. Astrid sues Manny, Mary, and the school district. Mary intends to countersue.

1. Who is the complainant?
   A. Manny   B. Mary   C. Astrid   D. Carlos

2. Which of the following is NOT a possible cause of action?
   A. Harassment
   B. Assault
   C. Negligence
   D. Breach of Contract

3. What key information is missing from the complaint?
   A. The name of the bullied student
   B. The location where Carlos was jumped
   C. The name of the high school principal
   D. The name of the police officer at the NYPD School Safety Unit who was originally notified on the issue

4. Is Mary obligated to countersue because she or her son, Manny, may have been involved in the assault against Carlos?
   A. Yes; she must answer the suit and countersue as required
   B. Yes; she must countersue to clear her son's name
   C. No; Mary is not obligated to countersue and can simply answer to the claims as alleged
   D. No; Mary is not obligated to countersue but she is obligated to countersue on Manny's behalf

5. Assume that Carlos and Manny are minors.
   What effect, if any, would this fact have on the lawsuit that is filed?
   A. The legal guardians of Carlos and Manny will need to file, and answer, the lawsuit on their behalf.
   B. Carlos and Manny do not need to appear in court.
   C. Minors cannot sue other people.
   D. The lawsuit is unaffected by their age.

6.

Mary Williams 1 Court Way Smithtown, NY 10170	Mary S. Williams 1 Court Way Smithtown, NY 10170	Mary S. Williams 1 Court Way Smith Town, NY 10170

   Which selection below accurately describes the addresses as listed above?
   A. All three addresses are the same.
   B. The first and the third address are the same.
   C. None of the addresses are the same.
   D. The second and third address are the same.

Questions 7-9.

DIRECTIONS: Questions 7 through 9 are to be answered on the basis of the following table.

Schedule – Judge Presser		
Petitioner	**Respondent**	**Status**
Williams	Smith	Dismissed with prejudice
Jones	Johnson	Continued
Adams	Doe	Dismissed with prejudice
Ash	Link	Adjourned
Lam	Garcia	Settled

7. How many cases were adjourned?
   A. 3   B. 1   C. 4   D. 5

8. In how many cases were money damages awarded by the judge?
   A. 0   B. 3   C. 4   D. 5

9. How many cases will be heard again?
   A. 2   B. 1   C. 3   D. 5

10. A warrant for the arrest of Benjamin Lang. Lang lives in Suffolk County, New York. What is recorded on the warrant?
    Lang's
    A. venue   B. domicile
    C. jurisdiction   D. subject matter jurisdiction

Questions 11-13.

DIRECTIONS: Questions 11 through 13 are to be answered on the basis of the following table.

455888912	455888812	455888912	455888812
Civil Court	Civil Court	Civil Court	Civil Court
Contract	Contract	Contract	Contract
Pam L. Williams	Pam Williams	Pam Williams	Pam L. Williams

11. Which selection below accurately describes the case captions as listed above?
    A. All of the captions are the same.
    B. Caption 1 and Caption 3 are the same.
    C. Caption 2 and Caption 4 are the same.
    D. None of the captions are the same.

11.____

12. Which digit above is dissimilar in two of the above captions?
    A. The seventh digit
    B. The fifth digit
    C. The sixth digit
    D. The eighth digit

12.____

13. The notation "contract" in each caption above describes the _____ of the case.
    A. Cause of action
    B. Remedy at issue
    C. Order of the court
    D. Disposition

13.____

14. Melinda was seen stealing money from a car on Atlantic Avenue in Brooklyn. Samuel witnessed the crime from his apartment and called the police. Officer Tang recorded the call in the police log. Samuel does not own a car and reported the crime anonymously. Later that same evening, Jeremy returned his car and found the passenger window had been broken and $500 was stolen from the glove compartment. Jeremy called the police to report the crime.
In the judge's docket, the petitioner of the case against Melinda is MOST likely
    A. Jeremy
    B. Samuel
    C. Officer Tang
    D. The petitioner is anonymous

14.____

15. Judge Oswald hears cases in the Surrogate Court.
Which of the following would NOT be in Judge Oswald's court calendar?
    A. Adoption
    B. Wills
    C. Estate and Probation
    D. Negligence

15.____

Questions 16-19.

DIRECTIONS: Questions 16 through 19 are to be answered on the basis of the following fact pattern.

Judge Laredo, Smith and Ora hear no-fault cases in the 10th Judicial District throughout the week. Judge Laredo hears cases the first Monday of each month. Judge Smith hears cases with amounts in dispute over $10,000 on Tuesday, Wednesday, and Friday. Judge Ora hears cases without amounts in dispute below $25,000 on Tuesdays only.

16. Geico and ABC Chiropractic are parties to a no-fault dispute with an amount in dispute of $8,500.
    If Judge Laredo is unavailable, what day can the case be heard?
    A. Wednesday B. Friday C. Monday D. Tuesday

17. Blue Health Medical and Progressive Insurance are parties to a no-fault dispute which is scheduled to be heard February 18th. Blue Health demands Progressive reimburse the provider $5,000 for the primary surgeon fees and $12,000 in assistant surgeon fees.
    Which judge will hear the matter and on which day?
    A. Judge Smith on Friday
    B. Judge Smith on Tuesday
    C. Judge Smith on Wednesday
    D. Judge Ora on Tuesday

18. A no-fault dispute is being heard on Monday, June 10th.
    Which statement below must be TRUE?
    A. The amount in dispute is above $10,000.
    B. The amount in dispute is less than $25,000.
    C. The amount in dispute is less than $10,000.
    D. Judge Laredo is hearing the case.

19. What information must be obtained in order to properly schedule the court calendar?
    A. The amount in dispute for each case
    B. The parties in each case
    C. Verification the dispute is "no-fault in nature"
    D. All of the above

20. A victim impact statement is an oral or _____ statement that may be read in court.
    A. recorded B. transcribed C. written D. visualized

21. The clerk in the Surrogates Court will need to have access to what information in the preparation of adoption hearings?
    A. Personal information of a child's current or prior legal guardian
    B. Emancipation petition documentation
    C. Deed or will
    D. Probate documentation

Questions 22-25.

DIRECTIONS: Questions 22 through 25 are to be answered on the basis of the following table.

Schedule – Judge Orlando			
Complainant/Plaintiff	Defendant	Case Type	Money Awarded
Williams	Smith	Civil	$5,000
Jones	Johnson	Criminal	No
Adams	Doe	Criminal	$10,000
Ash	Link	Civil	$15,000
Lam	Garcia	Civil	$25,000

22. What is the total amount of money damages from civil disputes? 22.____
    A. $45,000   B. $40,000   C. $5,000   D. 0

23. Which complainant/plaintiff was awarded less than $20,000? 23.____
    A. Williams, Adams, and Ash   B. Jones, Adams, and Ash
    C. Lam, Williams, and Jones   D. Jones, Adams, and Lam

24. How many criminal cases were heard by Judge Orlando? 24.____
    A. 4   B. 5   C. 2   D. 3

25. Which defendants are responsible for paying more than $10,000? 25.____
    A. Doe and Link   B. Link and Garcia
    C. John and Doe   D. Smith and Garcia

KEY (CORRECT ANSWERS)

1.	C	11.	D
2.	D	12.	A
3.	B	13.	A
4.	C	14.	A
5.	A	15.	D
6.	C	16.	D
7.	B	17.	D
8.	A	18.	D
9.	A	19.	D
10.	B	20.	C

21. A
22. A
23. A
24. C
25. B

TEST 2

DIRECTIONS: Each question or incomplete statement is followed by several suggested answers or completions. Select the one that BEST answers the question or completes the statement. *PRINT THE LETTER OF THE CORRECT ANSWER IN THE SPACE AT THE RIGHT.*

Questions 1-4.

DIRECTIONS: Questions 1 through 4 are to be answered on the basis of the following text.

After a lengthy trial with multiple ___1___, Jim was acquitted of armed robbery and conspiracy. On the other hand, his alleged partner, Bob, was ___2___ of armed robbery. The conspiracy charge was dropped against Bob since the 12-person ___3___ found he acted alone. Jim's attorney ___4___.

1. Fill in the blank for #1:
   A. witnesses   B. evidence   C. discretionary   D. turbulent

2. Fill in the blank for #2:
   A. guilty   B. convicted   C. indicted   D. surmised

3. Fill in the blank for #3:
   A. judge   B. spectator   C. jury   D. bailiff

4. Fill in the blank for #4:
   A. appealed   B. remanded   C. reversed   D. rescinded

Questions 5-10.

DIRECTIONS: Questions 5 through 10 are to be answered on the basis of the following table.

| Court Schedule - Tuesday ||||
Judge	Total Cases	Cases Dismissed	Cases with Money Awarded
Presser	10	2	X
O'Dell	5	5	
Williams	6	6	
Sasha	8	7	X

5. How many cases were awarded money damages from Judge Presser's calendar?
   A. 2   B. 8   C. 6   D. 10

6. How many cases were awarded money damages from Judge Sasha's calendar?
   A. 8   B. 7   C. 1   D. 0

7. How many cases were dismissed on Tuesday?
   A. 11   B. 20   C. 7   D. 10

8. How many cases were awarded money damages on Tuesday?
   A. 9   B. 8   C. 1   D. 10

9. Which judge heard the MOST cases on Tuesday?
   A. Presser   B. O'Dell   C. Williams   D. Sasha

10. Which judge heard the LEAST cases on Tuesday?
    A. Presser   B. O'Dell   C. Willliams   D. Sasha

Questions 11-15.

DIRECTIONS: Questions 11 through 15 are to be answered on the basis of the following text.

Judge Smith hears adoption cases on Fridays. Judge Clark hears criminal cases every weekday except Tuesday in the New York City Criminal Court. Judge Clark hears felony criminal cases on Tuesday in Supreme Court. Judge Amy hears felony criminal cases on Thursday in Supreme Court.

11. Daniel is being charged with the murder of his cousin, Jerrell.
    Which judge can hear the case and on what day?
    A. Judge Smith on Friday   B. Judge Clark on Monday
    C. Judge Amy on Tuesday   D. Judge Clark on Tuesday

12. Jamal lives in Staten Island with his sister, Tisha, and Tisha's boyfriend, Hunter. Hunter and Jamal do not get along and one day last January, Hunter and Jamal were involved in a physical altercation. Hunter and Jamal both allege that the other assault and battered the other.
    Which judge can hear the case and on what day?
    A. Judge Clark on Tuesday   B. Judge Amy on Thursday
    C. Judge Smith on Friday   D. Judge Clark on Monday

13. Assuming the crime of assault and battery are not felonies, in which court will Jamal and Hunter's dispute be heard?
    A. Supreme Court   B. Surrogates Court
    C. New York City Criminal Court   D. Small Claims Court

14. Assume that Tisha and Hunter have a six-year-old daughter.
    If Hunter is incarcerated for his role in the physical altercation with Jamal, which court would have jurisdiction over Hunter's trial?
    A. Surrogates Court   B. New York City Criminal Court
    C. Bronx Housing Court   D. Richmond County Civil Court

15. What day of the week are the MOST cases heard between all three judges?
    A. Monday   B. Thursday   C. Tuesday   D. Friday

Questions 16-19.

DIRECTIONS: Questions 16 through 19 are to be answered on the basis of the following table.

Caption #1	Caption #2	Caption #3	Caption #4
Case 12-908	Case 12-909	Case 12-910	Case 12-911
Bronx Housing Court	Civil Court	Civil Court	Surrogates Court
Landlord/Tenant	Assault	Breach of Contract	Guardianship
ABC Property Mgmt v. Sam Smith	Jim Jones v. Sam Hunt	Terrell Williams v. Daniel Tang	In re: Jane Doe

16. Which caption above contains an INCORRECT cause of action?
    A. 1   B. 2   C. 3   D. 4

17. When were the cases in each of the captions above initiated?
    A. 2015
    B. 2016
    C. 2012
    D. Unable to determine based on the information provided

18. Which case caption above corresponds to a matter that will NOT have monetary damages awarded?
    A. 1   B. 2   C. 3   D. 4

19. Which case caption has a matter involving an institutional, rather than an individual, petitioner?
    A. 1   B. 2   C. 3   D. 4

20. A pro se litigant wants to initiate a lawsuit against his intrusive neighbor. Assuming the pro se litigant prevails, which form should be served against the neighbor after the judgment is entered?
    A. Notice of entry   B. Notice of appeal
    C. Remand service   D. Process discovery

21. A(n) _____ is a hearing for the purpose of determining the amount of damages sue on a claim. The clerk can enter the request on the judge's calendar after the opposing party has defaulted.
    A. imposition   B. inquest   C. tardy notice   D. reversal

22. After a judgment is entered, it becomes enforceable for a period of time. For real property, a transcript of _____ is filed with the County Clerk which makes the judgment enforceable for a period of ten years.
    A. enforcement   B. judgment
    C. engagement   D. affidavit

23. Sensitive information must be _____ before it becomes public record.
    A. retained   B. reposed   C. redacted   D. recanted

4 (#2)

24. Service of process can be filed upon the individual or upon the _____. The affidavit of service will state the party that received the service.
    A. secretary of state
    B. guardian
    C. ad litem
    D. second most suitable person

24._____

25. A warrant can be issued to a sheriff or a marshal. The warrant clerk is responsible for reviewing the paperwork and ensuring that all is in order, including
    A. the names of the parties
    B. address of the premises
    C. the index number
    D. all of the above

25._____

KEY (CORRECT ANSWERS)

1.	A	11.	D
2.	B	12.	D
3.	C	13.	C
4.	A	14.	B
5.	B	15.	D
6.	C	16.	B
7.	B	17.	C
8.	A	18.	D
9.	A	19.	A
10.	B	20.	A

21.	B
22.	B
23.	C
24.	A
25.	D

TEST 3

DIRECTIONS: Each question or incomplete statement is followed by several suggested answers or completions. Select the one that BEST answers the question or completes the statement. *PRINT THE LETTER OF THE CORRECT ANSWER IN THE SPACE AT THE RIGHT.*

1. Supreme Court clerks need to be on notice when a(n) _____ is filed as a judge is not assigned until one that parties files this document and pays the filing fee. A case will never go to trial if this document is never filed. 1._____
   A. request for maintenance
   B. request for judicial intervention
   C. remediation
   D. arbitration

Questions 2-4.

DIRECTIONS: Questions 1 through 5 are to be answered on the basis of the following chart.

Row	Case Type	Court
1	Divorce	Supreme Court
2	Custody/Visitation	Family Court
3	Child Support	Family Court
4	Paternity	Family Court
5	When Someone Dies	Surrogates Court
6	Guardianship	Surrogate's Court
7	Name Change	Supreme Court
8	Housing	New York City Housing Court

2. Assume that you are advising a pro se litigant on the proper forms to file when representing him or herself. Where would John file a small estate affidavit? 2._____
   A. Family Court
   B. Supreme Court
   C. Surrogates Court
   D. New York Civil Court

3. Where would Tom's sister, Emmanuela, file a name change? 3._____
   A. Supreme Court
   B. Family Court
   C. Surrogates Court
   D. New York City Civil Court

4. Tara and her husband, Cassidy, share custody of their twin sons, Drake and Austin. Cassidy would like to petition the court for sole custody. Where would Cassidy file his petition? 4._____
   A. New York City Housing Court
   B. Supreme Court
   C. Family Court
   D. Surrogates Court

5. Richard is representing himself in a lawsuit against his landlord. Richard does not have the financial means to hire an attorney and would like to request a reduction in the court filing fees. Richard must file a request for a _____ which is made by filing a _____ and sworn _____ which explains his finances to the court.
   A. fee waiver; notice of motion; affirmation
   B. fee waiver, notice of motion, affidavit
   C. affidavit, notice of motion, fee waiver
   D. affidavit, fee waiver, notice of motion

Questions 6-10.

DIRECTIONS: Questions 6 through 10 are to be answered on the basis of the following text.

Daniel walks into this local supermarket after lunch and falls in one of the store aisles. Daniel lies on the floor – which is nearly empty – until one of the store managers finds him, helps him up, and offers to pay for his groceries. Daniel leaves the store bruised, but not seriously injured. Two days later, Daniel falls at another grocery store. This time, Daniel threatens to sue the grocery store. The second grocery store has heard about Daniel and is concerned that he is falsifying his injuries to gain sympathy and money. The second grocery store sues Daniel to get ahead of Daniel suing them.

6. Who is the plaintiff in the case?
   A. The first grocery store
   B. The second grocery store
   C. The grocery store manager
   D. Daniel

7. Which of the following is the MOST likely cause of action in a suit that Daniel initiates against the grocery store?
   A. Breach of contract
   B. Discrimination
   C. Negligence
   D. Assault

8. After the lawsuit has commenced, which party would respond or file an answer to the complaint?
   A. Daniel
   B. The first grocery store
   C. The second grocery store
   D. The grocery store manager

9. Which party is eligible to countersue?
   A. The first grocery store
   B. The second grocery store
   C. The grocery store manager
   D. Daniel

10. The lawsuit will likely be dismissed. Why?
    A. Daniel is clearly not exaggerating his injuries.
    B. Daniel has not sued either grocery store.
    C. The store manager did not take a report of Daniel's injuries.
    D. The first grocery store must sue Daniel first.

11. A settlement between parties is not a final and binding legal agreement until the _____ of settlement is signed by both parties.
    A. amendment   B. agreement   C. stipulation   D. simulation

12. Which of the following are appropriate reasons for filing an Order to Show Cause? 12.____
    A. Changing the terms of a court order
    B. Requesting the court to dismiss a case
    C. Bringing the case back to court for any reason
    D. All of the above

13. Which of the following is NOT an appropriate reason for filing an Order to Show Case? 13.____
    A. Asking for more time to do something previously agreed upon by court order
    B. Explaining why either party missed a court date
    C. Submitting financial information for a landlord/tenant dispute
    D. Fixing errors in a stipulation

Questions 14-17.

DIRECTIONS: Questions 14 through 17 are to be answered on the basis of the following text.

Judge Chin hears child neglect and abuse cases in Family Court on Mondays and Tuesdays. Judge Amy hears divorce cases on Mondays, Wednesdays, and Fridays. Judge Snell hears child support and visitation cases every day of the week except Thursday. Termination of parental rights, foster care placement, and other child support cases are scheduled on Thursdays only with any of the three judges.

14. Tim and Sarah would like to adjust their visitation schedule for their eight-year-old daughter, Samantha. They would like the courts to assist them with this issue as they have been unable to come to an agreement on their own. 14.____
    Which judge will hear the case and on what day?
    A. Judge Snell on Thursday   B. Judge Snell on Monday
    C. Judge Chin on Monday   D. Judge Chin on Friday

15. Amanda would like to file for emancipation from her parents. 15.____
    Which judge is MOST likely to hear her case?
    A. Judge Chin
    B. Judge Amy
    C. Judge Snell'
    D. Any of the judges can hear Amanda's case

16. Jimmy and Eva are legally separating. Which judge will hear their case and on what day? 16.____
    A. Judge Chin on Monday   B. Judge Snell on Monday
    C. Judge Amy on Monday   D. Judge Chin on Tuesday

17. The State of New York intends to file a case against Eric for the abuses and neglect of his daughter, Clare. Eric, however, is not Clare's legal guardian. Clare's legal guardian is her grandmother, Allison. Even though it is not clear that Clare has been neglected, the courts have found that Clare should be placed into foster care until it can be determined who the ultimate caregiver should be.
Which judge will MOST likely hear this case?
    A. Judge Amy
    B. Judge Chin
    C. Judge Snell
    D. Any of the judges can hear this case

Questions 18-25.

DIRECTIONS: Questions 18 through 25 are to be answered on the basis of the following chart.

Item	Fee
Obtaining an index number	$210
RJI	$95
Note of Issue	$30
Motion or Cross-Motion	$45
Demand for Jury Trial	$65
Voluntary Discontinuance	$35
Notice of Appeal	$65

18. What is the final cost to obtain an index number, demand a jury trial, and file a notice of appeal?
    A. $210   B. $35   C. $65   D. $310

19. What is the final cost to obtain an RJI and note of issue?
    A. $125   B. $95   C. $30   D. $65

20. Which of the following is MOST likely to be filed with an RJI?
    A. Demand for jury trial   B. Notice of appeal
    C. Voluntary discontinuance   D. Obtaining an index number

21. Which of the following is the MOST likely outcome of filing a voluntary discontinuance?
The case
    A. is automatically appealed   B. is dismissed
    C. is rescheduled   D. will be remanded

22. What is the final cost of filing a notice of appeal?
    A. $35   B. $65   C. $95   D. $120

23. What is the final cost of all items prior to filing a motion or cross-motion?
    A. $210   B. $95   C. $45   D. $335

24. Jamal would like to petition the court to compel discovery from his adversary and former friend, Bob. He would also like to speed up the date of trial by filing a demand for jury trial and RJI.
What is the final cost to do so?
   A. $160
   B. $95
   C. $65
   D. $205

24.____

25. What is the LEAST costly court document filing fee?
   A. Notice of motion
   B. Demand for jury trial
   C. Note of issue
   D. RJI

25.____

KEY (CORRECT ANSWERS)

1. B
2. C
3. A
4. C
5. B

6. B
7. C
8. A
9. D
10. B

11. C
12. D
13. C
14. B
15. D

16. C
17. D
18. D
19. A
20. D

21. B
22. B
23. D
24. D
25. C

TEST 4

DIRECTIONS: Each question or incomplete statement is followed by several suggested answers or completions. Select the one that BEST answers the question or completes the statement. *PRINT THE LETTER OF THE CORRECT ANSWER IN THE SPACE AT THE RIGHT.*

1. A lawsuit for money damages amounting to more than $25,000 can be heard in which court?
   A. Surrogates Court
   B. Supreme Court
   C. New York City Civil Court
   D. New York City Criminal Court

   1.____

2. Which of the following will NOT be on a Notice of Entry?
   A. Name of plaintiff
   B. Name of defendant
   C. Index number
   D. Social Security number

   2.____

3. Court clerks are prohibited from which of the following?
   A. Predicting the judgment of the court
   B. Explaining available options for a case or problem
   C. Providing past rulings
   D. Providing citations or copies of the law

   3.____

4. Court clerks are permitted to do all of the following EXCEPT
   A. provide forms with instructions
   B. instruct an individual on how to make a complaint
   C. analyze the law based on the specifics of a case
   D. describe court records and their availability

   4.____

5. Mary would like to sue her neighbor, Jacob, for money damages. Mary claims Jacob ran his car into Mary's garage door while it was down and caused $5,000 in damages. For claims below $1,000, the filing fee is $15, while the filing fee is $5 more for claims above $1,000.
   How much is Mary's filing fee?
   A. $15   B. $10   C. $20   D. $25

   5.____

Questions 6-10.

DIRECTIONS: Questions 6 through 10 are to be answered on the basis of the following table.

Schedule – Judge O'Neill		
Wednesday	**Thursday**	**Friday**
Continued	Dismissed with prejudice	Dismissed with prejudice
Continued	Adjourned	Continued
Settled	Dismissed with prejudice	Dismissed without prejudice
Settled	Continued	Settled
Settled	Continued	Settled

6. How many cases were adjourned this week?
   A. 5   B. 6   C. 1   D. 2

   6.____

85

7. How many cases settled this week?
   A. 5   B. 4   C. 3   D. 8

   7.____

8. How many cases were dismissed this week?
   A. 6   B. 4   C. 5   D. 7

   8.____

9. How many cases will likely be heard again or, in other words, how many cases can be re-filed or are otherwise continued?
   A. 6   B. 5   C. 7   D. 8

   9.____

10. Which day was Judge O'Neill the LEAST busy?
    A. Thursday   B. Friday
    C. Wednesday   D. Each day was equally busy

    10.____

Questions 11-15.

DIRECTIONS: Questions 11 through 15 are to be answered on the basis of the following text.

At Alex's arraignment, he pled ____1____ to the charge of driving under the influence and vehicular manslaughter. At trial, the prosecutor presented evidence from several ____2____ that testified Alex had a drinking problem. While Alex's defense attorneys ____3____ to that testimony and argued it was hearsay, the judge overruled those objections and allowed the testimony to be entered in the record as originally spoken. At the conclusion of the trial, Alex was found ____4____ and sentenced to community service.

11. Fill in the blank for #1:
    A. nolo   B. contendere   C. not guilty   D. guilty

    11.____

12. Fill in the blank for #2:
    A. witnesses   B. evidence   C. testimony   D. bearer

    12.____

13. Fill in the blank for #3:
    A. disagreed   B. objected   C. qualified   D. disclaimed

    13.____

14. Fill in the blank for #4:
    A. arraigned   B. protested   C. remanded   D. guilty

    14.____

15. An acquittal can also be recorded in court documentation as a finding of
    A. reversal   B. recusal   C. not guilty   D. remand

    15.____

16. Evidence must be found _____ before it can be marked and evaluated by the fact finder, either a judge or jury, in civil and criminal cases.
    A. relevant   B. redacted   C. qualified   D. admissible

    16.____

17. The party who seeks an appeal from a decision of a court is deemed a(n) _____ and is recorded in court documentation as such.
    A. petitioner   B. respondent   C. appellant   D. re-respondent

    17.____

18. How would a condominium be recorded in a bankruptcy proceeding?
    A. Real property
    B. Personal property
    C. Intangible asset
    D. chattel

19. Which of the following is LEAST likely to be recorded as a written statement describing one's legal and factual arguments?
    A. Attorney's brief
    B. Motion
    C. Summons
    D. Complaint

20. A lawsuit where one or more members of a large group of individuals sues on behalf of the other individuals in the large group is recorded as a _____ lawsuit.
    A. introductory   B. class action   C. municipality   D. winning

21. Jamal has filed for bankruptcy. After the trustee has reviewed Jamal's assets, the trustee proposes a plan to the court where Jamal promises property that he already owns to satisfy the major of his debt.
    The property Jamal owns that will satisfy the debt is recorded as
    A. demerits   B. collateral   C. debris   D. probate

22. Judge Presser has rendered Emilio's sentence for the charges of armed robbery and kidnapping. Emilio will serve 10 years for armed robbery and 12 years for kidnapping.
    If Emilio's total time in prison is 12 years, his sentence is recorded as
    A. consecutive
    B. demonstrative
    C. concurrent
    D. rebated

23. Assume the same facts as the previous question, but assume Emilio serves 22 years in prison.
    In this instance, his sentence is recorded as
    A. consecutive
    B. demonstrative
    C. concurrent
    D. rebated

24. A conviction can also be recorded in court records as a judgment of _____ against a defendant.
    A. guilt   B. remorse   C. retaliation   D. acquittal

25. In bankruptcy, Jamal sells his house to his mother for $5 in an effort to hide it from creditors who will require that he sell it to satisfy his debts.
    This sale is recorded as a
    A. fraudulent transfer
    B. falsified sale
    C. remarkable trade
    D. clawback trade

KEY (CORRECT ANSWERS)

1.	B		11.	C
2.	D		12.	A
3.	A		13.	B
4.	C		14.	D
5.	C		15.	C
6.	C		16.	D
7.	A		17.	C
8.	B		18.	A
9.	A		19.	C
10.	C		20.	B

21. B
22. C
23. A
24. A
25. A

READING COMPREHENSION
UNDERSTANDING AND INTERPRETING WRITTEN MATERIAL
EXAMINATION SECTION
TEST 1

DIRECTIONS: Each question or incomplete statement is followed by several suggested answers or completions. Select the one that BEST answers the question or completes the statement. *PRINT THE LETTER OF THE CORRECT ANSWER IN THE SPACE AT THE RIGHT.*

Questions 1-4.

DIRECTIONS: Questions 1 through 4 are to be answered SOLELY on the basis of the following passage.

Those engaged in the exercise of First Amendment rights by pickets, marches, parades, and open-air assemblies are not exempted from obeying valid local traffic ordinances. In a recent pronouncement, Mr. Justice Baxter, speaking for the Supreme Court, wrote:

The rights of free speech and assembly, while fundamental to our democratic society, still do not mean that everyone with opinions or beliefs to express may address a group at any public place and at any time. The constitutional guarantee of liberty implies the existence of an organized society maintaining public order, without which liberty itself would be lost in the excesses of anarchy. The control of travel on the streets is a clear example of governmental responsibility to insure this necessary order. A restriction in that relation, designed to promote the public convenience in the interest of all, and not susceptible to abuses of discriminatory application, cannot be disregarded by the attempted exercise of some civil rights which, in other circumstances, would be entitled to protection. One would not be justified in ignoring the familiar red light because this was thought to be a means of social protest. Governmental authorities have the duty and responsibility to keep their streets open and available for movement. A group of demonstrators could not insist upon the right to cordon off a street, or entrance to a public or private building, and allow no one to pass who did not agree to listen to their exhortations.

1. Which of the following statements BEST reflects Mr. Justice Baxter's view of the relationship between liberty and public order?

    A. Public order cannot exist without liberty.
    B. Liberty cannot exist without public order.
    C. The existence of liberty undermines the existence of public order.
    D. The maintenance of public order insures the existence of liberty.

2. According to the above passage, local traffic ordinances result from

    A. governmental limitations on individual liberty
    B. governmental responsibility to insure public order
    C. majority rule as determined by democratic procedures
    D. restrictions on expression of dissent

1.____

2.____

3. The above passage suggests that government would be acting improperly if a local traffic ordinance

   A. was enforced in a discriminatory manner
   B. resulted in public inconvenience
   C. violated the right of free speech and assembly
   D. was not essential to public order

4. Of the following, the MOST appropriate title for the above passage is

   A. THE RIGHTS OF FREE SPEECH AND ASSEMBLY
   B. ENFORCEMENT OF LOCAL TRAFFIC ORDINANCES
   C. FIRST AMENDMENT RIGHTS AND LOCAL TRAFFIC ORDINANCES
   D. LIBERTY AND ANARCHY

Questions 5-8

DIRECTIONS: Questions 5 through 8 are to be answered SOLELY on the basis of the following passage

On November 8, 1976, the Supreme Court refused to block the payment of Medicaid funds for elective abortions. The Court's action means that a new Federal statute that bars the use of Federal funds for abortions unless abortion is necessary to save the life of the mother will not go into effect for many months, if at all.

A Federal District Court in Brooklyn ruled the following month that the statute was unconstitutional and ordered that Federal reimbursement for the costs of abortions continue on the same basis as reimbursements for the costs of pregnancy and childbirth-related services.

Technically, what the Court did today was to deny a request by Senator Howard Ramsdell and others for a stay blocking enforcement of the District Court order pending appeal. The Court's action was a victory for New York City. The City's Health and Hospitals Corporation initiated one of the two lawsuits challenging the new statute that led to the District Court's decision. The Corporation also opposed the request for a Supreme Court stay of that decision, telling the Court in a memorandum that a stay would subject the Corporation to a *grave and irreparable injury.*

5. According to the above passage, it would be CORRECT to state that the Health and Hospitals Corporation

   A. joined Senator Ramsdell in his request for a stay
   B. opposed the statute which limited reimbursement for the cost of abortions
   C. claimed that it would experience a loss if the District Court order was enforced
   D. appealed the District Court decision

6. The above passage indicates that the Supreme Court acted in DIRECT response to

   A. a lawsuit initiated by the Health and Hospitals Corporation
   B. a ruling by a Federal District Court
   C. a request for a stay
   D. the passage of a new Federal statute

7. According to the above passage, it would be CORRECT to state that the Supreme Court
   A. blocked enforcement of the District Court order
   B. refused a request for a stay to block enforcement of the Federal statute
   C. ruled that the new Federal statute was unconstitutional
   D. permitted payment of Federal funds for abortion to continue

8. Following are three statements concerning abortion that might be correct:
   I. Abortion costs are no longer to be Federally reimbursed on the same basis as those for pregnancy and childbirth
   II. Federal funds have not been available for abortions except to save the life of the mother
   III. Medicaid has paid for elective abortions in the past

   According to the passage above, which of the following CORRECTLY classifies the above statements into those that are true and those that are not true?

   A. I is true, but II and III are not.
   B. I and III are true, but II is not.
   C. I and II are true, but III is not.
   D. III is true, but I and II are not.

Questions 9-12.

DIRECTIONS: Questions 9 through 12 are to be answered SOLELY on the basis of the following passage.

A person may use physical force upon another person when and to the extent he reasonably believes such to be necessary to defend himself or a third person from what he reasonably believes to be the use or imminent use of unlawful physical force by such other person, unless (a) the latter's conduct was provoked by the actor himself with intent to cause physical injury to another person; or (b) the actor was the initial aggressor; or (c) the physical force involved is the product of a combat by agreement not specifically authorized by law.

A person may not use deadly physical force upon another person under the circumstances specified above unless (a) he reasonably believes that such other person is using or is about to use deadly physical force. Even in such case, however, the actor may not use deadly physical force if he knows he can, with complete safety, as to himself and others avoid the necessity of doing so by retreating; except that he is under no duty to retreat if he is in his dwelling and is not the initial aggressor; or (b) he reasonably believes that such other person is committing or attempting to commit a kidnapping, forcible rape, or forcible sodomy.

9. Jones and Smith, who have not met before, get into an argument in a tavern. Smith takes a punch at Jones, but misses. Jones then hits Smith on the chin with his fist. Smith falls to the floor and suffers minor injuries.
   According to the above passage, it would be CORRECT to state that _____ justified in using physical force.

   A. only Smith was
   B. only Jones was
   C. both Smith and Jones were
   D. neither Smith nor Jones was

10. While walking down the street, Brady observes Miller striking Mrs. Adams on the head with his fist in an attempt to steal her purse.
    According to the above passage, it would be CORRECT to state that Brady would

    A. not be justified in using deadly physical force against Miller since Brady can safely retreat
    B. be justified in using physical force against Miller but not deadly physical force
    C. not be justified in using physical force against Miller since Brady himself is not being attacked
    D. be justified in using deadly physical force

11. Winters is attacked from behind by Sharp, who attempts to beat up Winters with a blackjack. Winters disarms Sharp and succeeds in subduing him with a series of blows to the head. Sharp stops fighting and explains that he thought Winters was the person who had robbed his apartment a few minutes before, but now realizes his mistake.
    According to the above passage, it would be CORRECT to state that

    A. Winters was justified in using physical force on Sharp only to the extent necessary to defend himself
    B. Winters was not justified in using physical force on Sharp since Sharp's attack was provoked by what he believed to be Winters' behavior
    C. Sharp was justified in using physical force on Winters since he reasonably believed that Winters had unlawfully robbed him
    D. Winters was justified in using physical force on Sharp only because Sharp was acting mistakenly in attacking him

12. Roberts hears a noise in the cellar of his home, and, upon investigation, discovers an intruder, Welch. Welch moves towards Roberts in a threatening manner, thrusts his hand into a bulging pocket, and withdraws what appears to be a gun. Roberts thereupon strikes Welch over the head with a golf club. He then sees that the *gun* is a toy. Welch later dies of head injuries. According to the above passage, it would be CORRECT to state that Roberts was

    A. justified in using deadly physical force because he reasonably believed Welch was about to use deadly physical force
    B. not justified in using deadly physical force
    C. justified in using deadly physical force only because he did not provoke Welch's conduct
    D. justified in using deadly physical force only because he was not the initial aggressor

Questions 13-16.

DIRECTIONS: Questions 13 through 16 are to be answered SOLELY on the basis of the following passage.

From the beginning, the Supreme Court has supervised the fairness of trials conducted by the Federal government. But the Constitution, as originally drafted, gave the court no such general authority in state cases. The court's power to deal with state cases comes from the Fourteenth Amendment, which became part of the Constitution in 1868. The crucial provision forbids any state to *deprive any person of life, liberty, or property without due process of law.*

The guarantee of *due process* would seem, at the least, to require fair procedure in criminal trials. But curiously the Supreme Court did not speak on the question for many decades. During that time, however, the due process clause was interpreted to bar *unreasonable* state economic regulations, such as minimum wage laws.

In 1915, there came the case of Leo M. Frank, a Georgian convicted of murder in a trial that he contended was dominated by mob hysteria. Historians now agree that there was such hysteria, with overtones of anti-semitism.

The Supreme Court held that it could not look past the findings of the Georgia courts that there had been no mob atmosphere at the trial. Justices Oliver Wendell Holmes and Charles Evans Hughes dissented, arguing that the constitutional guarantee would be *a barren one* if the Federal courts could not make their own inferences from the facts.

In 1923, the case of Moore v. Dempsey involved five Arkansas Blacks convicted of murder and sentenced to death in a community so aroused against them that at one point they were saved from lynching only by Federal troops. Witnesses against them were said to have been beaten into testifying.

The court, though not actually setting aside the convictions, directed a lower Federal court to hold a habeas corpus hearing to find out whether the trial had been fair, or whether the whole proceeding had been *a mask—that counsel, jury, and judge were swept to the fatal end by an irresistible wave of public passion.*

13. According to the above passage, the Supreme Court's INITIAL interpretation of the Fourteenth Amendment

    A. protected state supremacy in economic matters
    B. increased the scope of Federal jurisdiction
    C. required fair procedures in criminal trials
    D. prohibited the enactment of minimum wage laws

14. According to the above passage, the Supreme Court in the Frank case

    A. denied that there had been mob hysteria at the trial
    B. decided that the guilty verdict was supported by the evidence
    C. declined to question the state court's determination of the facts
    D. found that Leo Frank had not received *due process*

15. According to the above passage, the dissenting judges in the Frank case maintained that

    A. due process was an empty promise in the circumstances of that case
    B. the Federal courts could not guarantee certain provisions of the Constitution
    C. the Federal courts should not make their own inferences from the facts in state cases
    D. the Supreme Court had rendered the Constitution *barren*

16. Of the following, the MOST appropriate title for the above passage is 16.____
    A. THE CONDUCT OF FEDERAL TRIALS
    B. THE DEVELOPMENT OF STATES' RIGHTS: 1868-1923
    C. MOORE V. DEMPSEY: A CASE STUDY IN CRIMINAL JUSTICE
    D. DUE PROCESS-THE EVOLUTION OF A CONSTITUTIONAL CORNERSTONE

Questions 17-20.

DIRECTIONS: Questions 17 through 20 are to be answered SOLELY on the basis of the following passage.

The difficulty experienced in determining which party has the burden of proving payment or non-payment is due largely to a lack of consistency between the rules of pleading and the rules of proof. In some cases, a plaintiff is obligated by a rule of pleading to allege non-payment on his complaint, yet is not obligated to prove non-payment on the trial. An action upon a contract for the payment of money will serve as an illustration. In such a case, the plaintiff must allege non-payment in his complaint, but the burden of proving payment on the trial is upon the defendant. An important and frequently cited case on this problem is Conkling v. Weatherwax. In that case, the action was brought to establish and enforce a legacy as a lien upon real property. The defendant alleged in her answer that the legacy had been paid. There was no witness competent to testify for the plaintiff to show that the legacy had not been paid. Therefore, the question of the burden of proof became of primary importance since, if the plaintiff had the burden of proving non-payment, she must fail in her action; whereas if the burden of proof was on the defendant to prove payment, the plaintiff might win. The Court of Appeals held that the burden of proof was on the plaintiff. In the course of his opinion, Judge Vann attempted to harmonize the conflicting cases on this subject, and for that purpose formulated three rules. These rules have been construed and applied to numerous subsequent cases. As so construed and applied, these may be summarized as follows:

Rule 1. In an action upon a contract for the payment of money only, where the complaint does not allege a balance due over and above all payments made, the plaintiff must allege nonpayment in his complaint, but the burden of proving payment is upon the defendant. In such a case, payment is an affirmative defense which the defendant must plead in his answer. If the defendant fails to plead payment, but pleads a general denial instead, he will not be permitted to introduce evidence of payment.

Rule 2. Where the complaint sets forth a balance in excess of all payments, owing to the structure of the pleading, burden is upon the plaintiff to prove his allegation. In this case, the defendant is not required to plead payment as a defense in his answer but may introduce evidence of payment under a general denial.

Rule 3. When the action is not upon contract for the payment of money, but is upon an obligation created by operation of law, or is for the enforcement of a lien where non-payment of the amount secured is part of the cause of action, it is necessary both to allege and prove the fact of nonpayment.

17. In the above passage, the case of Conkling v. Weatherwax was cited PRIMARILY to illustrate

    A. a case where the burden of proof was on the defendant to prove payment
    B. how the question of the burden of proof can affect the outcome of a case
    C. the effect of a legacy as a lien upon real property
    D. how conflicting cases concerning the burden of proof were harmonized

18. According to the above passage, the pleading of payment is a defense in Rule(s)

    A. 1, but not Rules 2 and 3
    B. 2, but not Rules 1 and 3
    C. 1 and 3, but not Rule 2
    D. 2 and 3, but not Rule 1

19. The facts in Conkling v. Weatherwax CLOSELY resemble the conditions described in

    A. Rule #1
    B. Rule #2
    C. Rule #3
    D. none of the rules

20. The MAJOR topic of the above passage may BEST be described as

    A. determining the ownership of property
    B. providing a legal definition
    C. placing the burden of proof
    D. formulating rules for deciding cases

Questions 21-25.

DIRECTIONS: Questions 21 through 25 are to be answered SOLELY on the basis of the following passage.

The law is quite clear that evidence obtained in violation of Section 605 of the Federal Communications Act is not admissible in Federal court. However, the law as to the admissibility of evidence in state court is far from clear. Had the Supreme Court of the United States made the wiretap exclusionary rule applicable to the states, such confusion would not exist.

In the case of Alton v. Texas, the Supreme Court was called upon to determine whether wiretapping by state and local officers came within the proscription of the Federal statute and, if so, whether Section 605 required the same remedies for its vindication in state courts. In answer to the first question, Mr. Justice Minton, speaking for the court, flatly stated that Section 605 made it a federal crime for anyone to intercept telephone messages and divulge what he learned. The court went on to say that a state officer who testified in state court concerning the existence, contents, substance, purport, effect, or meaning of an intercepted conversation violated the Federal law and committed a criminal act. In regard to the second question, how-ever, the Supreme Court felt constrained by due regard for federal-state relations to answer in the negative. Mr. Justice Minton stated that the court would not presume, in the absence of a clear manifestation of congressional intent, that Congress intended to supersede state rules of evidence.

Because the Supreme Court refused to apply the exclusionary rule to wiretap evidence that was being used in state courts, the states respectively made this decision for themselves. According to hearings held before a congressional committee in 1975, six states authorize wiretapping by statute, 33 states impose total bans on wiretapping, and 11 states have no definite statute on the subject. For examples of extremes, a statute in Pennsylvania will be compared with a statute in New York.

The Pennsylvania statute provides that no communications by telephone or telegraph can be intercepted without permission of both parties. It also specifically prohibits such interception by public officials and provides that evidence obtained cannot be used in court.

The lawmakers in New York, recognizing the need for legal wire-tapping, authorized wiretapping by statute. A New York law authorizes the issuance of an ex parte order upon oath or affirmation for limited wiretapping. The aim of the New York law is to allow court-ordered wiretapping and to encourage the testimony of state officers concerning such wiretapping in court. The New York law was found to be constitutional by the New York State Supreme Court in 1975. Other states, including Oregon, Maryland, Nevada, and Massachusetts, enacted similar laws which authorize court-ordered wiretapping.

To add to this legal disarray, the vast majority of the states, including New Jersey and New York, permit wiretapping evidence to be received in court even though obtained in violation of the state laws and of Section 605 of the Federal act. However, some states, such as Rhode Island, have enacted statutory exclusionary rules which provide that illegally procured wiretap evidence is incompetent in civil as well as criminal actions.

21. According to the above passage, a state officer who testifies in New York State court concerning the contents of a conversation he overheard through a court-ordered wire-tap is in violation of _____ law.

    A. state law but not federal
    B. federal law but not state
    C. federal law and state
    D. neither federal nor state

22. According to the above passage, which of the following statements concerning states statutes on wiretapping is CORRECT?

    A. The number of states that impose total bans on wiretapping is three times as great as the number of states with no definite statute on wiretapping.
    B. The number of states having no definite statute on wiretapping is more than twice the number of states authorizing wiretapping.
    C. The number of states which authorize wiretapping by statute and the number of states having no definite statute on wiretapping exceed the number of states imposing total bans on wiretapping.
    D. More states authorize wiretapping by statute than impose total bans on wiretapping.

23. Following are three statements concerning wiretapping that might be valid:
    I. In Pennsylvania, only public officials may legally intercept telephone communications.
    II. In Rhode Island, evidence obtained through an illegal wiretap is incompetent in criminal, but not civil, actions.
    III. Neither Massachusetts nor Pennsylvania authorizes wiretapping by public officials.

    According to the above passage, which of the following CORRECTLY classifies these statements into those that are valid and those that are not?

    A. I is valid, but II and III are not.
    B. II is valid, but I and III are not.
    C. II and III are valid, but I is not.
    D. None of the statements is valid.

24. According to the above passage, evidence obtained in violation of Section 605 of the Federal Communications Act is inadmissible in

    A. federal court but not in any state courts
    B. federal court and all state courts
    C. all state courts but not in federal court
    D. federal court and some state courts

25. In regard to state rules of evidence, Mr. Justice Minton expressed the Court's opinion that Congress

    A. intended to supersede state rules of evidence, as manifested by Section 605 of the Federal Communications Act
    B. assumed that federal statutes would govern state rules of evidence in all wiretap cases
    C. left unclear whether it intended to supersede state rules of evidence
    D. precluded itself from superseding state rules of evidence through its regard for federal-state relations

KEY (CORRECT ANSWERS)

1. B
2. B
3. A
4. C
5. B

6. C
7. D
8. D
9. B
10. B

11. A
12. A
13. D
14. C
15. A

16. D
17. B
18. A
19. C
20. C

21. B
22. A
23. D
24. D
25. C

TEST 2

DIRECTIONS: Each question or incomplete statement is followed by several suggested answers or completions. Select the one that BEST answers the question or completes the Statement. *PRINT THE LETTER OF THE CORRECT ANSWER IN THE SPACE AT THE RIGHT.*

Questions 1-3.

DIRECTIONS: Questions 1 through 3 are to be answered SOLELY on the basis of the following passage.

    The State Assembly has passed a bill that would require all state agencies, public authorities, and local governments to refuse bids in excess of $2,000 from any foreign firm or corporation. The only exceptions to this outright prohibition against public buying of foreign goods or services would be for products not available in this country, goods of a quality unobtainable from an American supplier, and products using foreign materials that are *substantially* manufactured in the United States.

    This bill is a flagrant violation of the United States' officially espoused trade principles. It would add to the costs of state and local governments. It could provoke retaliatory action from many foreign governments against the state and other American producers, and foreign governments would be fully entitled to take such retaliatory action under the General Agreement on Tariffs and Trade, which the United States has signed.

    The State Senate, which now has the Assembly bill before it, should reject this protectionist legislation out of enlightened regard for the interests of the taxpayers and producers of the State—as well as for those of the nation and its trading partners generally. In this time of unemployment and international monetary disorder, the State—with its reputation for intelligent and progressive law-making—should avoid contributing to what could become a tidal wave of protectionism here and overseas.

1. Under the requirements of the bill passed by the State Assembly, a bid from a foreign manufacturer in excess of $2,000 can be accepted by a state agency or local government only if it meets which one of the following requirements?
The

    A. bid is approved individually by the State Legislature
    B. bidder is willing to accept payment in United States currency
    C. bid is for an item of a quality unobtainable from an American supplier
    D. bid is for an item which would be more expensive if it were purchased from an American supplier

1.____

2. The author of the above passage feels that the bill passed by the State Assembly should be

    A. passed by the State Senate and put into effect
    B. passed by the State Senate but vetoed by the Governor
    C. reintroduced into the State Assembly and rejected
    D. rejected by the State Senate

2.____

3. The author of the above passage calls the practice of prohibiting purchase of products manufactured by foreign countries

   A. prohibition
   B. protectionism
   C. retaliatory action
   D. isolationism

Questions 4-7.

DIRECTIONS: Questions 4 through 7 are to be answered SOLELY on the basis of the following passage.

    Data processing is by no means a new invention. In one form or another, it has been carried on throughout the entire history of civilization. In its most general sense, data processing means organizing data so that it can be used for a specific purpose-a procedure commonly known simply as *record-keeping* or *paperwork*. With the development of modern office equipment, and particularly with the recent introduction of computers, the techniques of data processing have become highly elaborate and sophisticated, but the basic purpose remains the same: Turning raw data into useful information.

    The key concept here is usefulness. The data, or input, that is to be processed can be compared to the raw material that is to go into a manufacturing process. The information, or output, that results from data processing—like the finished product of a manufacturer—should be clearly usable. A collection of data has little value unless it is converted into information that serves a specific function.

4. The expression *paperwork,* as it is used in this passage,

   A. shows that the author regards such operations as a waste of time
   B. has the same general meaning as *data processing*
   C. refers to methods of record-keeping that are no longer in use
   D. indicates that the public does not understand the purpose of data processing

5. The above passage indicates that the use of computers has

   A. greatly simplified the clerical work in an office
   B. led to more complicated systems for the handling of data
   C. had no effect whatsoever on data processing
   D. made other modern office machines obsolete

6. Which of the following BEST expresses the basic principle of data processing as it is described in the above passage?

   A. Input-processing-output
   B. Historical record-keeping-modern techniques -specific functions
   C. Office equipment-computer-accurate data
   D. Raw material-manufacturer-retailer

7. According to the above passage, data processing may be described as

   A. a new management technique
   B. computer technology
   C. information output
   D. record-keeping

Questions 8-10.

DIRECTIONS: Questions 8 through 10 are to be answered SOLELY on the basis of the following passage.

A loan receipt is an instrument devised to permit the insurance company to bring an action against the wrongdoer in the name of the insured despite the fact that the insured no longer has any financial interest in the outcome. It provides, in effect, that the amount of the loss is advanced to the insured as a loan which is repayable only up to the extent of any recovery made from the wrongdoer. The insured further agrees to enter and prosecute suit against the wrongdoer in his own name. Such a receipt substitutes a loan for a payment for the purpose of permitting the insurance company to press its action against the wrongdoer in the name of the insured.

8. According to the above passage, the purpose behind the use of a loan receipt is to 8._____

   A. guarantee that the insurance company gets repayment from the person insured
   B. insure repayment of all expenditures to the named insured
   C. make it possible for the insurance company to sue in the name of the policyowner
   D. prevent the wrongdoer from escaping the natural consequences of his act

9. According to the above passage, the amount of the loan which must be paid back to the insurance company equals but does NOT exceed the amount 9._____

   A. of the loss
   B. on the face of the policy
   C. paid to the insured
   D. recovered from the wrongdoer

10. According to the above passage, by giving a loan receipt, the person insured agrees to 10._____

    A. a suit against the wrongdoer in his own name
    B. forego any financial gain from the outcome of the suit
    C. institute an action on behalf of the insurance company
    D. repay the insurance company for the loan received

Questions 11-12.

DIRECTIONS: Questions 11 and 12 are to be answered SOLELY on the basis of the following passage.

Open air markets originally came into existence spontaneously when groups of pushcart peddlers congregated in spots where business was good. Good business induced them to return to these spots daily and, thus, unofficial open air markets arose. These peddlers paid no fees, and the city received no revenue from them. Confusion and disorder reigned in these unsupervised markets; the earliest arrivals secured the best locations, unless or until forcibly ejected by stronger or tougher peddlers. Although the open air markets supplied a definite need in the community, there were many detrimental factors involved in their operation. They were unsightly, created unsanitary conditions in market streets by the deposit of garbage and waste and were a definite obstruction to traffic, as well as a fire hazard.

11. On the basis of the above passage, the MOST accurate of the following statements is:

    A. Each peddler in the original open air markets had his own fixed location.
    B. Open air markets were originally organized by means of agreements between groups of pushcart peddlers.
    C. The locations of these markets depended upon the amount of business the vendors were able to do.
    D. There was confusion and disorder in these open air markets because the peddlers were not required to pay any fees to the city.

12. Of the following, the MOST valid implication which can be made on the basis of the above passage is that the

    A. detrimental aspect of the operations of open air markets was the probable reason for the creation of enclosed markets under the supervision of the Department of Markets
    B. open air markets could not supply any community need without proper supervision
    C. original open air markets were good examples of the operation of fair competition in business
    D. possibility of obtaining a source of revenue was probably the most important reason for the city's ultimate undertaking of the supervision of open air markets

Questions 13-14.

DIRECTIONS: Questions 13 and 14 are to be answered SOLELY on the basis of the following passage.

A person who displays on his window, door, or in his place of business words or letters in Hebraic characters other than the word *kosher,* or any sign, emblem, insignia, six-pointed star, symbol or mark in simulation of same, without displaying in conjunction there-with in English letters of at least the same size as such characters, signs, emblems, insignia or marks, the words *we sell kosher meat and food only* or *we sell non-kosher meat and food only* or *we sell both kosher and non-kosher meat and food,* as the case may be, is guilty of a misdemeanor. Possession of non-kosher meat and food in any place of business advertising the sale of kosher meat and food only is presumptive evidence that the person in possession exposes the same for sale with intent to defraud, in violation of the provisions of this section.

13. Of the following, the MOST valid implication that can be made on the basis of the above passage is that a person who

    A. displays on his window a six-pointed star in addition to the word *kosher* in Hebraic letters is guilty of intent to defraud
    B. displays on his window the word *kosher* in Hebraic characters intends to indicate that he has only kosher food for sale
    C. sells both kosher and non-kosher food in the same place of business is guilty of a misdemeanor
    D. sells only that type of food which can be characterized as neither kosher nor non-kosher, such as fruit and vegetables, without an explanatory sign in English is guilty of intent to defraud

14. Of the following, the one which would constitute a violation of the rules of the above passage is a case in which a person 14._____

    A. displays the word *kosher* on his window in Hebraic letters has only kosher meat and food in the store but has some non-kosher meat in the rear of the establishment
    B. selling both kosher and non-kosher meat and food uses words in Hebraic letters, other than the word *kosher,* on his window and a sign of the same size letters in English stating *we sell both kosher and non-kosher meat and food*
    C. selling only kosher meat and food uses words in Hebraic letters, other than the word *kosher,* on his window and a sign of the same size letters in English stating *we sell kosher meat and food only*
    D. selling only non-kosher meat and food displays a six-pointed star on his window and a sign of the same size letters in English stating *we sell only non-kosher meat and food*

Questions 15-16.

DIRECTIONS: Questions 15 and 16 are to be answered SOLELY on the basis of the following passage.

COMMODITIES IN GLASS BOTTLES OR JARS

The contents of the bottle may be stated in terms of weight or of fluid measure, the weight being indicated in terms of pounds and ounces and the fluid measure being indicated in terms of gallons, quarts, pints, half-pints, gills, or fluid ounces. When contents are liquid, the amount should not be stated in terms of weight. The marking indicating content is to be on a tag attached to the bottle or upon a label. The letters shall be in bold-faced type at least one-ninth of an inch (1/9") in height for bottles or jars having a capacity of a gill, half-pint, pint, or multiples of a pint, and letters at least three-sixteenths of an inch (3/16") in height for bottles of other capacities, on a part of the tag or label free from other printing or ornamentation, leaving a clear space around the marking which indicates the contents.

15. Of the following, the one which does NOT meet the requirements of the above passage is a 15._____

    A. bottle of cooking oil with a label stating *contents—16 fluid ounces* in appropriate sized letters
    B. bottle of vinegar with a label stating *contents—8 ounces avoir.* in appropriate sized letters
    C. glass jar filled with instant coffee with a label stating *contents—1 lb. 3 ozs. avoir.* in appropriate sized letters
    D. glass jar filled with liquid bleach with a label stating *contents—1 quart* in appropriate sized letters

16. Of the following, the one which does meet the requirements of the above passage is a 16._____

    A. bottle filled with a low-calorie liquid sweetener with a label stating *contents—3 fluid ounces* in letters 1/12" high
    B. bottle filled with ammonia solution for cleaning with a label stating *contents—1 pint* in letters 1/10" high

C. jar filled with baking powder with a label stating *contents—$\frac{1}{2}$ pint* in letters $\frac{1}{4}$" high

D. jar filled with hard candy with a label stating *contents—1 lb. avoir.* in letters $\frac{1}{2}$" high

Question 17.

DIRECTIONS: Question 17 is to be answered SOLELY on the basis of the information contained in the following passage.

DEALERS IN SECOND HAND DEVICES

1. It shall be unlawful for any person to engage in or conduct the business of dealing in, trading in, selling, receiving, or repairing condemned, rebuilt, or used weighing or measuring devices without a permit therefor.

2. Such permit shall expire on the twenty-eighth day of February next succeeding the date of issuance thereof.

3. Every person engaged in the above business, within five days after the making of a repair, or the sale and delivery of a repaired, rebuilt, or used weighing or measuring device, shall serve notice in writing on the commissioner giving the name and address of the person for whom the repair has been made or to whom a repaired, rebuilt, or used weighing or measuring device has been sold or delivered, and shall include a statement that such device has been so altered, repaired, or rebuilt as to conform to the regulations of the department.

17. According to the above passage, the MOST accurate of the following statements is:

    A. A permit issued to engage in the business mentioned above, first issued on April 23, 1968, expired on February 28, 1969.
    B. A rebuilt or repaired weighing or measuring device should not operate with less error than the tolerances permitted by the regulations of the department.
    C. If a used scale in good condition is sold, it is not necessary for the seller to notify the commissioner of the name and address of the buyer.
    D. There is a difference in the time required to notify the commissioner of a repair or of a sale of a repaired device.

Questions 18-19.

DIRECTIONS: Questions 18 and 19 are to be answered SOLELY on the basis of the following passage.

    A. It shall be unlawful for any person, firm, or corporation to sell or offer for sale at retail for use in internal combustion engines in motor vehicles any gasoline unless such seller shall post and keep continuously posted on the individual pump or other dispensing device from which such gasoline is sold or offered for sale a sign or placard not less than seven inches in height and eight inches in width nor larger than twelve inches in height and twelve inches in width and stating clearly in numbers of uniform size the selling price or prices per gallon of such gasoline so sold or offered for sale from such pump or other dispensing device.

B. The amount of governmental tax to be collected in connection with the sale of such gasoline shall be stated on such sign or placard and separately and apart from such selling price or prices.

18. The one of the following price signs posted on a gasoline pump which would be in violation of the above passage is a sign _____ square inches in size and _____ inches high.

    A. 144; 12   B. 84; 7   C. 72; 12   D. 60; 8

19. According to the above passage, the LEAST accurate of the following statements is:

    A. Gasoline may be sold from a dispensing device other than a pump.
    B. If two different pumps are used to sell the same grade of gasoline, a price sign must appear on each pump.
    C. The amount of governmental tax and the price of the gasoline must not be stated on the same sign.
    D. The sizes of the numbers used on a sign to indicate the price of gasoline must be the same.

Questions 20-21.

DIRECTIONS: Questions 20 and 21 are to be answered SOLELY on the basis of the following passage.

In all systems of weights and measures based on one or more arbitrary fundamental units, the concrete representation of the unit in the form of a standard is necessary, and the construction and preservation of such a standard is a matter of primary importance. Therefore, it is essential that the standard should be so constructed as to be as nearly permanent and invariable as human ingenuity can contrive. The reference of all measures to an original standard is essential for their correctness, and such a standard must be maintained and preserved in its integrity by some responsible authority which is thus able to provide against the use of false weights and measures. Accordingly, from earliest times, standards were constructed and preserved under the direction of kings and priests, and the temples were a favorite place for their deposit. Later, this duty was assumed by the government, and today we find the integrity of standards of weights and measures safeguarded by international agreement.

20. Of the following, the MOST valid implication which can be made on the basis of the above passage is that

    A. fundamental units of systems of weights and measures should be represented by quantities so constructed that they are specific and constant
    B. in the earliest times, standards were so constructed that they were as permanent and invariable as modern ones
    C. international agreement has practically relieved the U.S. government of the necessity of preserving standards of weights and measures
    D. the preservation of standards is of less importance than the ingenuity used in their construction

21. Of the following, the MOST appropriate title for the above passage is   21.___

    A. THE CONSTRUCTION AND PRESERVATION OF STANDARDS OF WEIGHTS AND MEASURES
    B. THE FIXING OF RESPONSIBILITY FOR THE ESTABLISHMENT OF STANDARDS OF WEIGHTS AND MEASURES
    C. THE HISTORY OF SYSTEMS OF WEIGHTS AND MEASURES
    D. THE VALUE OF PROPER STANDARDS IN PROVIDING CORRECT WEIGHTS AND MEASURES

Questions 22-23.

DIRECTIONS: Questions 22 and 23 are to be answered SOLELY on the basis of the following passage.

Accurate weighing and good scales insure that excess is not given just for the sake of good measure. No more striking example of the fundamental importance of correct weighing to the business man is found than in the simple and usual relation where a charge or value is obtained by multiplying a weight by a unit price. For example, a scale may weigh *light*, that is, the actual quantity delivered is in excess by 1 percent. The actual result is that the seller taxes himself. If his profit is supposed to be 10 percent of total sales, an overweight of 1 percent represents 10 percent of that profit. Under these conditions, the situation is as though the seller were required to pay a sales tax equivalent to what he is taxing himself.

22. Of the following, the MOST valid implication which can be made on the basis of the above passage is that   22.___

    A. consistent use of scales that weigh *light* will reduce sellers' profits
    B. no good businessman would give any buyer more than the weight required even if his scale is accurate
    C. the kind of situation described in the above passage could not arise if sales were being made of merchandise sold by the yard
    D. the use of incorrect scales is one of the reasons causing governments to impose sales taxes

23. According to the above passage, the MOST accurate of the following statements is: 23.___

    A. If his scale weighs *light* by an amount of 2 percent, the seller would deliver only 98 pounds when 100 pounds was the amount agreed upon.
    B. If the seller's scale weighs *heavy*, the buyer will receive an amount in excess of what he intended to purchase.
    C. If the seller's scale weighs *light* by an amount of 1 percent, a buyer who agreed to purchase 50 pounds of merchandise would actually receive $50 \frac{1}{2}$ pounds.
    D. The use of a scale which delivers an amount which is in excess of that required is an example of deliberate fraud.

Questions 24-25.

DIRECTIONS: Questions 24 and 25 are to be answered SOLELY on the basis of the following passage.

Food shall be deemed to be misbranded:
1. If its labeling is false or misleading in any particular.

2. If any word, statement, or other information required by or under authority of this article to appear on the label or labeling is not prominently placed thereon with such conspicuousness (as compared with other words, statements, designs, or devices in the labeling) and in such terms as to render it likely to be read and understood by the ordinary individual under customary conditions of purchase and use.

3. If it purports to be or is represented as a food for which a standard of quality has been prescribed and its quality falls below such standard, unless its label bears a statement that it falls below such standard.

24. According to the above passage, the MOST accurate of the following statements is:

    A. A food may be considered misbranded if the label contains a considerable amount of information which is not required.
    B. If a consumer purchased one type of canned food, although he intended to buy another, the food is probably misbranded.
    C. If a food is used in large amounts by a group of people of certain foreign origin, it can be considered misbranded unless the label is in the foreign language with which they are familiar.
    D. The required information on a label is likely to be in larger print than other information which may appear on it.

25. According to the above passage, the one of the following foods which may be considered to be misbranded is a

    A. can of peaches with a label which carries the brand name of the packer but states *Below Standard in Quality*
    B. can of vegetables with a label on which is printed a shield which states *U.S. Grade B*
    C. package of frozen food which has some pertinent information printed on it in very small type which a customer cannot read and which the store manager cannot read when asked to do so by the customer
    D. package of margarine of the same size as the usual package of butter, kept near the butter, but clearly labeled as margarine

KEY (CORRECT ANSWERS)

1. C
2. D
3. B
4. B
5. B

6. A
7. D
8. C
9. D
10. A

11. C
12. A
13. B
14. A
15. B

16. D
17. A
18. C
19. C
20. A

21. D
22. A
23. C
24. D
25. C

READING COMPREHENSION
UNDERSTANDING AND INTERPRETING WRITTEN MATERIAL
EXAMINATION SECTION
TEST 1

DIRECTIONS: Each question or incomplete statement is followed by several suggested answers or completions. Select the one that BEST answers the question or completes the statement. *PRINT THE LETTER OF THE CORRECT ANSWER IN THE SPACE AT THE RIGHT.*

Questions 1-4.

DIRECTIONS: Questions 1 through 4 are to be answered SOLELY on the basis of the information given in the paragraph below.

Abandoned cars – with tires gone, chrome stripped away, and windows smashed – have become a common sight on the city's streets. In 2000, more than 72,000 were deposited at curbs by owners who never came back, an increase of 15,000 from the year before and more than 30 times the number abandoned a decade ago. In January 2001, the city Environmental Protection Administrator asked the State Legislature to pass a law requiring a buyer of a new automobile to deposit $100 and an owner of an automobile at the time the law takes effect to deposit $50 with the State Department of Motor Vehicles. In return, they would be given a certificate of deposit which would be passed on to each succeeding owner. The final owner would get the deposit money back if he could present proof that he has disposed of his car *in an environmentally acceptable manner.* The Legislature has given no indication that it plans to rush ahead on the matter.

1. The number of cars abandoned in the city streets in 1990 was MOST NEARLY

    A. 2,500
    B. 12,000
    C. 27,500
    D. 57,000

2. The proposed law would require a person who owned a car bought before the law was passed to deposit

    A. $100 with the State Department of Motor Vehicles
    B. $50 with the Environmental Protection Administration
    C. $100 with the State Legislature
    D. $50 with the State Department of Motor Vehicles

3. The proposed law would require the State to return the deposit money ONLY when the

    A. original owner of the car shows proof that he sold it
    B. last owner of the car shows proof that he got rid of the car in a satisfactory way
    C. owner of a car shows proof that he has transferred the certificate of deposit to the next owner
    D. last owner of a car returns the certificate of deposit

4. The MAIN idea or theme of the above article is that

   A. a proposed new law would make it necessary for car owners in the State to pay additional taxes
   B. the State Legislature is against a proposed law to require deposits from automobile owners to prevent them from abandoning their cars
   C. the city is trying to find a solution for the increasing number of cars abandoned on its streets
   D. to pay for the removal of abandoned cars the city's Environmental Protection Administrator has asked the State to fine automobile owners who abandon their vehicles

Questions 5-7.

DIRECTIONS: Questions 5 through 7 are to be answered SOLELY on the basis of the information given in the paragraph below.

The regulations applying to parking meters provide that the driver is required to deposit the appropriate coin immediately upon parking and it is illegal for him to return at a later period to extend the parking time. If there is unused time on a parking meter, another car may be parked for a period not to exceed the unused time without the deposit of a coin. Operators of commercial vehicles are not required to deposit coins while loading or unloading expeditiously. By definition, a vehicle is considered parked even though there is a driver at the wheel and the meter must be used by the driver of such car.

5. According to the above paragraph, the regulations applying to parking meters do NOT

   A. allow the driver of a parked vehicle to stay in his car
   B. consider any loading or unloading of a vehicle as parking
   C. make any distinction between an unoccupied car and one with the driver at the wheel
   D. permit a driver who has parked a car at a meter with unused parking time to put a coin in the meter

6. According to the above paragraph, it is a violation of the parking meter regulations to

   A. load and unload slowly
   B. park commercial vehicles except for loading and unloading
   C. put a second coin in the meter in order to park longer
   D. use a parking space at any time without depositing a coin

7. The above paragraph CLEARLY indicates

   A. the number of minutes a vehicle may be parked
   B. the value of the coin that is to be put in the meter
   C. what is meant by a commercial vehicle
   D. when a car may be parked free

Questions 8-13.

DIRECTIONS: Questions 8 through 13 are to be answered on the basis of the information given in the paragraph below.

There are many types of reports. One of these is the field report, which requests information specified and grouped under columns or headings. A detailed, printed form is often used in submitting field reports. However, these printed, standardized forms provide a limited amount of space. The field man is required to make the decision as to how much of the information he has should go directly into the report and how much should be left for clarification if and when he is called in to explain a reported finding. In many instances, the addition of a short explanation of the finding might relieve the reader of the report of the necessity to seek an explanation. Therefore, the basic factual information asked for by the printed report form should often be clarified by some simple explanatory statement. If this is done, the reported finding becomes meaningful to the reader of the report who is far from the scene of the subject matter dealt with in the report. The significance of that which is reported finds its expression in the adoption of certain policies, improvements, or additions essential to furthering the effectiveness of the program.

8. According to the above paragraph, the field report asks for

   A. a detailed statement of the facts
   B. field information which comes under the heading of technical data
   C. replies to well-planned questions
   D. specific information in different columns

9. According to the above paragraph, the usual printed field report form

   A. does not have much room for writing
   B. is carefully laid out
   C. is necessary for the collection of facts
   D. usually has from three to four columns

10. According to the above paragraph, the man in the field MUST decide if

    A. a report is needed at all
    B. he should be called in to explain a reported finding
    C. he should put all the information he has into the report
    D. the reader of the report is justified in seeking an explanation

11. According to the above paragraph, the man in the field may be required to

    A. be acquainted with the person or persons who will read his report
    B. explain the information he reports
    C. give advice on specific problems
    D. keep records of the amount of work he completes

12. According to the above paragraph, the value of an explanatory statement added to the factual information reported in the printed forms is that it

    A. allows the person making the report to express himself briefly
    B. forces the person making the report to think logically
    C. helps the report reader understand the facts reported
    D. makes it possible to turn in the report later

13. According to the above paragraph, the importance of the information given by the field man in his report is shown by the

    A. adoption of policies and improvements
    B. effectiveness of the field staff
    C. fact that such a report is required
    D. necessary cost studies to back up the facts

Questions 14-15.

DIRECTIONS: Questions 14 and 15 are to be answered on the basis of the information contained in the following paragraph.

    The driver of the collection crew shall at all times remain in or on a department vehicle in which there is revenue. In the event such driver must leave the vehicle, he shall designate one of the other members of the crew to remain in or on the vehicle. The member of the crew so designated by the driver shall remain in or on the vehicle until relieved by the driver or another member of the crew. The vehicle may be left unattended only when there is no revenue contained therein provided, however, that in that event the vehicle shall be locked. The loss of any vehicle or any of its contents, including revenue, resulting from any deviation from this rule, shall be the responsibility of the member or members of crew who shall be guilty of such deviation.

14. The vehicle of a collection crew may be left with no one in it only if

    A. it is locked
    B. there is a crew member nearby
    C. there is no money in it
    D. there is only one member in the crew

15. If money is stolen from an unattended vehicle of a collection crew, the employee held responsible is the

    A. driver
    B. one who left the vehicle unattended
    C. one who left the vehicle unlocked
    D. one who relieved the driver

Questions 16-18.

DIRECTIONS: Questions 16 through 18 are to be answered SOLELY on the basis of the information given in the paragraph below.

    Safety belts provide protection for the passengers of a vehicle by preventing them from crashing around inside if the vehicle is involved in a collision. They operate on the principle similar to that used in the packaging of fragile items. You become a part of the vehicle package, and you are kept from being tossed about inside if the vehicle is suddenly decelerated. Many injury-causing collisions at low speeds, for example at city intersections, could have been injury-free if the occupants had fastened their safety belts. There is a double advantage to the driver in that it not only protects him from harm, but prevents him from being yanked away from the wheel, thereby permitting him to maintain control of the car.

16. The principle on which seat belts work is that

    A. a car and its driver and passengers are fragile
    B. a person fastened to the car will not be thrown around when the car slows down suddenly
    C. the driver and passengers of a car that is suddenly decelerated will be thrown forward
    D. the driver and passengers of an automobile should be packaged the way fragile items are packaged

17. We can assume from the above passage that safety belts should be worn at all times because you can never tell when

    A. a car will be forced to turn off onto another road
    B. it will be necessary to shift into low gear to go up a hill
    C. you will have to speed up to pass another car
    D. a car may have to come to a sudden stop

18. Besides preventing injury, an ADDITIONAL benefit from the use of safety belts is that

    A. collisions are fewer
    B. damage to the car is kept down
    C. the car can be kept under control
    D. the number of accidents at city intersections is reduced

Questions 19-24.

DIRECTIONS: Questions 19 through 24 are to be answered on the basis of the following reading passage covering Procedures For Patrol.

PROCEDURES FOR PATROL

The primary function of all Parking Enforcement Agents assigned to patrol duty shall be to patrol assigned areas and issue summonses to violators of various sections of the City Traffic Regulations, which sections govern the parking or operation of vehicles. Parking Enforcement Agents occasionally may be called upon to distribute educational pamphlets and perform other work, at the discretion of the Bureau Chief.

Each Agent on patrol duty will be assigned a certain area (or areas) to be patrolled. These areas will be assigned during the daily roll call. Walking Cards will describe the street locations of the patrol and the manner in which the patrol is to be walked.

A Traffic Department vehicle will be provided for daily patrol assignments when necessary.

Each Agent shall accomplish an assigned field patrol in the following manner:

   a. Start each patrol at the location specified on the daily patrol sheet, and proceed as per walking instructions.
   b. Approach each metered space being utilized (each metered space in which a vehicle is parked). If the meter shows the expired flag, the member of the force shall prepare and affix a summons to the vehicle parked at meter.

c. Any vehicle in violation of any regulation governing the parking, standing, stopping, or movement of vehicles will be issued a summons.
d. No summons will be issued to a vehicle displaying an authorized vehicle identification plate of the Police Department unless the vehicle is parked in violation of the No Standing, No Stopping, Hydrant, Bus Stop, or Double Parking Regulations. Identification plates for Police Department automobiles are made of plastic and are of rectangular shape, 10 3/4" long, 3 3/4" high, black letters and numerals on a white background. The words POLICE DEPT. are printed on the face with the identification number. Identification plates for private automobiles are the same size and shape as those used on Police Department automobiles.

An Agent on patrol, when observing a person *feeding* a street meter (placing an additional coin in a meter so as to leave the vehicle parked for an additional period) shall prepare and affix a summons to the vehicle.

An Agent on patrol shall note on a computer card each missing or defective, out of order, or otherwise damaged meter.

19. Of the following, the work which the Parking Enforcement Agent performs MOST often is

    A. issuing summonses for parking violations
    B. distributing educational pamphlets
    C. assisting the Bureau Chief
    D. driving a city vehicle

20. The area to be covered by a Parking Enforcement Agent on patrol is

    A. determined by the Police Department
    B. regulated by the city Traffic Regulations
    C. marked off with red flags
    D. described on Walking Cards

21. A Parking Enforcement Agent reports a broken meter by

    A. issuing a summons
    B. making a mark on a computer card
    C. raising the flag on the broken meter
    D. attending a daily roll call

22. With respect to the use of an automobile for patrol duty,

    A. Parking Enforcement Agents must supply their own cars for patrol
    B. automobiles for patrol will be supplied by the Police Department
    C. Parking Enforcement Agents are permitted to park in a bus stop
    D. department vehicles will be provided when required for patrol

23. Parking Enforcement Agents sometimes issue summonses to drivers for *feeding* a street meter in violation of parking regulations.
    Which one of the following situations describes such a violation?
    A driver

    A. has moved from one metered space to another
    B. has parked next to a Police Department No Standing sign
    C. is parked by a meter which shows 30 minutes time still remaining
    D. has used a coin to reset the meter after his first time period expired

24. Vehicles displaying an authorized vehicle identification plate of the Police Department are allowed to park at expired meters.
Which one of the following statements describes the proper size of identification plates for private automobiles used for police work?
They

   A. are 10 3/4" long and 3 3/4" high
   B. have white letters and numerals on a black background
   C. are 3 3/4" long and 10 3/4" high
   D. have black letters and numerals on a white background

24._____

Questions 25-30.

DIRECTIONS: Questions 25 through 30 are to be answered on the basis of the following reading passage covering the Operation of Department Motor Vehicles.

OPERATION OF DEPARTMENT MOTOR VEHICLES

When operating a Traffic Department motor vehicle, a member of the force must show every courtesy to other drivers, obey all traffic signs and traffic regulations, obey all other lawful authority, and handle the vehicle in a manner which will foster safety practices in others and create a favorable impression of the Bureau, the Department, and the City. The operator and passengers MUST use the safety belts.

Driving Rules

   a. DO NOT operate a mechanically defective vehicle.
   DO NOT race engine on starting.
   DO NOT tamper with mechanical equipment.
   DO NOT run engine if there is an indication of low engine oil pressure, overheating, or no transmission oil.

   b. When parking on highway, all safety precautions must be observed.

   c. When parking in a garage or parking field, observe a maximum speed of 5 miles per hour. Place shift lever in park or neutral position, effectively apply hand brake, then shut off all ignition and light switches to prevent excess battery drain, and close all windows.

Reporting Defects

   a. Report all observed defects on Drivers' Vehicle Defect Card and on Monthly Vehicle Report Form 49 in sufficient detail so a mechanic can easily locate the source of trouble.
   b. Enter vehicle road service calls and actual time of occurrence on Monthly Vehicle Report.

Reporting Accidents

Promptly report all facts of each accident as follows: For serious accidents, including those involving personal injury, call your supervisor as soon as possible. Give all the appropriate information about the accident to your supervisor. Record vehicle registration information, including the name of the registered owner, the state, year, and serial number, and the classification marking on the license plates. Also record the operator's license number and other identifying information, and, if it applies, the injured person's age and sex. Give a full description of how the accident happened, and what happened following the accident, including the vehicles in collision, witnesses, police badge number, hospital, condition of road surface, time of day, weather conditions, location (near, far, center of intersection), and damage.

Repairs to Automobiles

When a Department motor vehicle requires repairs that cannot be made by the operator, or requires replacement of parts or accessories (including tires and tubes), or requires towing, the operator shall notify the District Commander.

When a Departmental motor vehicle is placed out of service for repairs, the Regional Commander shall assign another vehicle, if available.

Daily Operator's Report

The operator of a Department automobile shall keep a daily maintenance record of the vehicle, and note any unusual occurrences, on the Daily Operator's Report.

25. Parking Enforcement Agents who are assigned to operate Department motor vehicles on patrol are expected to

    A. disregard the posted speed limits to save time
    B. remove their seat belts on short trips
    C. show courtesy to other drivers on the road
    D. take the right of way at all intersections

26. The driver of a Department motor vehicle should

    A. leave the windows open when parking the vehicle in a garage
    B. drive the vehicle at approximately 10 miles per hour in a parking field
    C. be alert for indication of low engine oil pressure and overheated engine
    D. start a cold vehicle by racing the engine for 5 minutes

27. The reason that all defects on a Department vehicle that have been observed by its driver should be noted on a Monthly Vehicle Report Form 49 is:

    A. This action will foster better safety practices among other Agents
    B. The source of the defect may be located easily by a trained mechanic
    C. All the facts of an accident will be reported promptly
    D. The District Commander will not have to make road calls

28. If the driver of a Department vehicle is involved in an accident, an Accident Report should be made out. This Report should include a full description of how the accident happened.
   Which of the following statements would PROPERLY belong in an Accident Report?

   A. The accident occurred at the intersection of Broadway and 42nd Street.
   B. The operator of the Department motor vehicle replaced the windshield wiper.
   C. The vehicle was checked for gas and water before the patrol began.
   D. A bus passed two parked vehicles.

29. When a Department vehicle is disabled, whom should the operator notify?
   The

   A. Traffic Department garage
   B. Assistant Bureau Chief
   C. Police Department
   D. District Commander

30. The PROPER way for an operator of a Department vehicle to report unusual occurrences with respect to the operation of the vehicle is to

   A. follow the same procedures as for reporting a defect
   B. request the Regional Commander to assign another vehicle
   C. phone the Bureau Chief as soon as possible
   D. make a note of the circumstances on the Daily Operator's Report

KEY (CORRECT ANSWERS)

1.	A	16.	B
2.	D	17.	D
3.	B	18.	C
4.	C	19.	A
5.	C	20.	D
6.	C	21.	B
7.	D	22.	D
8.	D	23.	D
9.	A	24.	A
10.	C	25.	C
11.	B	26.	C
12.	C	27.	B
13.	A	28.	A
14.	C	29.	D
15.	B	30.	D

TEST 2

DIRECTIONS: Each question or incomplete statement is followed by several suggested answers or completions. Select the one that BEST answers the question or completes the statement. *PRINT THE LETTER OF THE CORRECT ANSWER IN THE SPACE AT THE RIGHT.*

Questions 1-4.

DIRECTIONS: Questions 1 through 4 are to be answered SOLELY on the basis of the information contained in the following passage.

Of those arrested in the city in 2003 for felonies or misdemeanors, only 32% were found guilty of any charge. Fifty-six percent of such arrestees were acquitted or had their cases dismissed. 11% failed to appear for trial, and 1% received other dispositions. Of those found guilty, only 7.4% received any sentences of over one year in jail. Only 50% of those found guilty were sentenced to any further time in jail. When considered with the low probability of arrests for most crimes, these figures make it clear that the crime control system in the city poses little threat to the average criminal. Delay compounds the problem. The average case took four appearances for disposition after arraignment. Twenty percent of all cases took eight or more appearances to reach a disposition. Forty-four percent of all cases took more than one year to disposition.

1. According to the above passage, crime statistics for 2003 indicate that   1.____

   A. there is a low probability of arrests for all crimes in the city
   B. the average criminal has much to fear from the law in the city
   C. over 10% of arrestees in the city charged with felonies or misdemeanors did not show up for trial
   D. criminals in the city are less likely to be caught than criminals in the rest of the country

2. The percentage of those arrested in 2003 who received sentences of over one year in jail amounted to MOST NEARLY   2.____

   A. .237   B. 2.4   C. 23.7   D. 24.0

3. According to the above passage, the percentage of arrestees in 2003 who were found guilty was   3.____

   A. 20% of those arrested for misdemeanors
   B. 11% of those arrested for felonies
   C. 50% of those sentenced to further time in jail
   D. 32% of those arrested for felonies or misdemeanors

4. According to the above paragraph, the number of appearances after arraignment and before disposition amounted to   4.____

   A. an average of four
   B. eight or more in 44% of the cases
   C. over four for cases which took more than a year
   D. between four and eight for most cases

Questions 5-6.

DIRECTIONS: Questions 5 and 6 are to be answered on the basis of the following paragraph.

A person who, with the intent to deprive or defraud another of the use and benefit of property or to appropriate the same to the use of the taker, or of any other person other than the true owner, wrongfully takes, obtains or withholds, by any means whatever, from the possession of the true owner or of any other person any money, personal property, thing in action, evidence of debt or contract, or article of value of any kind, steals such property and is guilty of larceny.

5. This definition from the Penal Law has NO application to the act of 5._____

   A. fraudulent conversion by a vendor of city sales tax money collected from purchasers
   B. refusing to give proper change after a purchaser has paid for an article in cash
   C. receiving property stolen from the rightful owner
   D. embezzling money from the rightful owner

6. According to the above paragraph, an auto mechanic who claimed to have a lien on an automobile for completed repairs and refused to surrender possession until the bill was paid 6._____

   A. *cannot* be charged with larceny because his repairs increased the value of the car
   B. *can* be charged with larceny because such actual possession can be construed to include intent to deprive the owner of use of the car
   C. *cannot* be charged with larceny because the withholding is temporary and such possession is not an evidence of debt
   D. *cannot* be charged with larceny because intent to defraud is lacking

Questions 7-12.

DIRECTIONS: Questions 7 through 12 are to be answered on the basis of the information given in the passage below. Assume that all questions refer to the same state described in the passage.

The courts and the police consider an *offense* as any conduct that is punishable by a fine or imprisonment. Such offenses include many kinds of acts—from behavior that is merely annoying, like throwing a noisy party that keeps everyone awake, all the way up to violent acts like murder. The law classifies offenses according to the penalties that are provided for them. In one state, minor offenses are called *violations*. A violation is punishable by a fine of not more than $250 or imprisonment of not more than 15 days, or both. The annoying behavior mentioned above is an example of a violation. More serious offenses are classified as *crimes*. Crimes are classified by the kind of penalty that is provided. A *misdemeanor* is a crime that is punishable by a fine of not more than $1,000 or by imprisonment of not more than 1 year, or both. Examples of misdemeanors include stealing something with a value of $100 or less, turning in a false alarm, or illegally possessing less than 1/8 of an ounce of a dangerous drug. A *felony* is a criminal offense punishable by imprisonment of more than 1 year. Murder is clearly a felony.

7. According to the above passage, any act that is punishable by imprisonment or by a fine is called a(n)

   A. offense B. violation C. crime D. felony

8. According to the above passage, which of the following is classified as a crime?

   A. Offense punishable by 15 days imprisonment
   B. Minor offense
   C. Violation
   D. Misdemeanor

9. According to the above passage, if a person guilty of burglary can receive a prison sentence of 7 years or more, burglary would be classified as a

   A. violation B. misdemeanor
   C. felony D. violent act

10. According to the above passage, two offenses that would BOTH be classified as misdemeanors are

    A. making unreasonable noise, and stealing a $90 bicycle
    B. stealing a $75 radio, and possessing 1/16 of an ounce of heroin
    C. holding up a bank, and possessing 1/4 of a pound of marijuana
    D. falsely reporting a fire, and illegally double-parking

11. The above passage says that offenses are classified according to the penalties provided for them.
    On the basis of clues in the passage, who probably decides what the maximum penalties should be for the different kinds of offenses?

    A. The State lawmakers B. The City police
    C. The Mayor D. Officials in Washington, D.C.

12. Of the following, which BEST describes the subject matter of the passage?

    A. How society deals with criminals
    B. How offenses are classified
    C. Three types of criminal behavior
    D. The police approach to offenders

Questions 13-20.

DIRECTIONS: Questions 13 through 20 are to be answered SOLELY on the basis of the following passage.

Auto theft is prevalent and costly. In 2005, 486,000 autos valued at over $500 million were stolen. About 28 percent of the inhabitants of Federal prisons are there as a result of conviction of interstate auto theft under the Dyer Act. In California alone, auto thefts cost the criminal justice system approximately $60 million yearly.

The great majority of auto theft is for temporary use rather than resale, as evidenced by the fact that 88 percent of autos stolen in 2005 were recovered. In Los Angeles, 64 percent of stolen autos that were recovered were found within two days, and about 80 percent within a week. Chicago reports that 71 percent of the recovered autos were found within four miles of the point of theft. The FBI estimates that 8 percent of stolen cars are taken for the purpose of stripping them for parts, 12 percent for resale, and 5 percent for use in another crime. Auto thefts are primarily juvenile acts. Although only 21 percent of all arrests for nontraffic offenses in 2005 were of individuals under 18 years of age, 63 percent of auto theft arrests were of persons under 18. Auto theft represents the start of many criminal careers; in an FBI sample of juvenile auto theft offenders, 41 percent had no prior arrest record.

13. In the above passage, the discussion of the reasons for auto theft does NOT include the percent of

   A. autos stolen by prior offenders
   B. recovered stolen autos found close to the point of theft
   C. stolen autos recovered within a week
   D. stolen autos which were recovered

14. Assuming the figures in the above passage remain constant, you may logically estimate the cost of auto thefts to the California criminal justice system over a five-year period beginning in 2005 to have been about _____ million.

   A. $200   B. $300   C. $440   D. $500

15. According to the above passage, the percent of stolen autos in Los Angeles which were not recovered within a week was _____ percent.

   A. 12   B. 20   C. 29   D. 36

16. According to the above passage, MOST auto thefts are committed by

   A. former inmates of Federal prisons
   B. juveniles
   C. persons with a prior arrest record
   D. residents of large cities

17. According to the above passage, MOST autos are stolen for

   A. resale
   B. stripping of parts
   C. temporary use
   D. use in another crime

18. According to the above passage, the percent of persons arrested for auto theft who were under 18

   A. equals nearly the same percent of stolen autos which were recovered
   B. equals nearly two-thirds of the total number of persons arrested for nontraffic offenses
   C. is the same as the percent of persons arrested for nontraffic offenses who were under 18
   D. is three times the percent of persons arrested for nontraffic offenses who were under 18

19. An APPROPRIATE title for the above passage is

   A. HOW CRIMINAL CAREERS BEGIN
   B. RECOVERY OF STOLEN CARS
   C. SOME STATISTICS ON AUTO THEFT
   D. THE COSTS OF AUTO THEFT

20. Based on the above passage, the number of cars taken for use in another crime in 2005 was

   A. 24,300   B. 38,880   C. 48,600   D. 58,320

Questions 21-22.

DIRECTIONS: Questions 21 and 22 are to be answered SOLELY on the basis of the following paragraph.

If the second or third felony is such that, upon a first conviction, the offender would be punishable by imprisonment for any term less than his natural life, then such person must be sentenced to imprisonment for an indeterminate term, the minimum of which shall be not less than one-half of the longest term prescribed upon a first conviction, and the maximum of which shall be not longer than twice such longest term, provided, however, that the minimum sentence imposed hereunder upon such second or third felony offender shall in no case be less than five years; except that where the maximum punishment for a second or third felony offender hereunder is five years or less, the minimum sentence must be not less than two years.

21. According to the above paragraph, a person who has a second felony conviction shall receive as a sentence for that second felony an indeterminate term

   A. not less than twice the minimum term prescribed upon a first conviction as a maximum
   B. not less than one-half the maximum term of his first conviction as a minimum
   C. not more than twice the minimum term prescribed upon a first conviction as a minimum
   D. with a maximum of not more than twice the longest term prescribed for a first conviction for this crime

22. According to the above paragraph, if the term for this crime for a first offender is up to three years, the possible indeterminate term for this crime as a second or third felony shall have a _____ of not _____ than _____ years.

   A. minimum; less; five
   B. maximum; more; five
   C. minimum; less; one and one-half
   D. maximum; less; six

23. A statute states: *A person who steals an article worth $1,000 or less where no aggravating circumstances accompany the act is guilty of petit larceny. If the article is worth more than $1,000, it may be grand larceny.*
   If all you know is that Edward Smith stole an article worth $1,000, it may reasonably be said that

   A. Smith is guilty of petit larceny
   B. Smith is guilty of grand larceny
   C. Smith is guilty of neither petit larceny nor grand larceny
   D. precisely what charge will be placed against Smith is uncertain

Questions 24-25.

DIRECTIONS: Questions 24 and 25 are to be answered on the basis of the following section of a law.

A person who, after having been three times convicted within this state of felonies or attempts to commit felonies, or under the law of any other state, government, or country, of crimes which if committed within this state would be felonious, commits a felony, other than murder, first or second degree, or treason, within this state, shall be sentenced upon conviction of such fourth, or subsequent, offense to imprisonment in a state prison for an indeterminate term the minimum of which shall be not less than the maximum term provided for first offenders for the crime for which the individual has been convicted, but, in any event, the minimum term upon conviction for a felony as the fourth or subsequent, offense shall be not less than fifteen years, and the maximum thereof shall be his natural life.

24. Under the terms of the above law, a person must receive the increased punishment therein provided if

   A. he is convicted of a felony and has been three times previously convicted of felonies
   B. he has been three times previously convicted of felonies, regardless of the nature of his present conviction
   C. his fourth conviction is for murder, first or second degree, or treason
   D. he has previously been convicted three times of murder, first or second degree, or treason

25. Under the terms of the above law, a person convicted of a felony for which the penalty is imprisonment for a term not to exceed ten years, and who has been three times previously convicted of felonies in this state, shall be sentenced to a term, the MINIMUM of which shall be

   A. 10 years   B. 15 years
   C. indeterminate   D. his natural life

KEY (CORRECT ANSWERS)

1. C
2. B
3. D
4. A
5. C

6. D
7. A
8. D
9. C
10. B

11. A
12. B
13. A
14. B
15. B

16. B
17. C
18. D
19. C
20. A

21. D
22. C
23. D
24. A
25. B

BASIC FUNDAMENTALS OF RECORD KEEPING

TABLE OF CONTENTS

	Page
Instructional Objectives	1
Content	1
Introduction	1
Filing Systems	2
Filing Methods	3
Miscellaneous Office Records	5
Data Processing	6
Processing the Data	6
Control Systems	7
Summary	8
Learning Activities	8
Management Activities	8
Evaluation Questions	9
Answer Key	10

BASIC FUNDAMENTALS OF RECORD KEEPING

Instructional Objectives
1. Ability to identify the characteristics of an effective record keeping system
2. Ability to explain the need for accurate, carefully maintained records in governmental agencies
3. Ability to identify the types of records that a governmental agency would maintain
4. Ability to develop a basic competence in alphabetical filing as well as an understanding of the variations in alphabetical filing rules and methods utilized in governmental agencies
5. Ability to recognize and utilize the various systems of filing in addition to (or in conjunction with) the alphabetical system
6. Ability to develop skill in finding information in office files, reference materials and agency manuals
7. Ability to develop a system of keeping track of the materials that have been removed from the files for study, microfilming or updating
8. Ability to describe the advantages of using microfilm for keeping records
9. Ability to analyze and determine the proper use of automated record keeping systems, such as the computer

Content

Introduction

From the birth certificate to the death certificate, everyone's lives are governed by records. The birth certificate verifies the individual's age, and will determine when he will enter public school, assume adult responsibilities and privileges, and be eligible to collect Social Security retirement benefits. School records will usually have direct bearing upon the individual's occupation. Federal and state income tax records will be established on the individual, as well as a record of marriage licenses, car licenses, and driver's licenses. This list of records ends with a death certificate which will enable the deceased's heirs to obtain his life insurance.

Public-service agencies, like individuals, are governed to a large extent by records of various sorts. Almost everyone who works in the field of public service will come in contact with different kinds of records and materials. Even the new employee may actually be involved in record keeping activities, or he may need to know about where different public records are kept, or how to find the necessary materials to assist in record keeping.

There is one basic reason for keeping or filing any records of valuable material – so that they may be found quickly when needed. In addition, there are basically two reasons for wanting to find materials – to verify or prove past actions or events, and to obtain information needed for planning future activities.

Materials to be filed in many public-service agencies may include letters, reports of many kinds (technical, financial, client interactions, marketing analyses), memorandums, copies of communications, contracts and other legal documents, price lists, clippings from newspapers and other published materials, checks, statements, receipts, bills, and other financial records.

One of the most important aspects of record keeping is the need for legibility. Records that cannot be read are of little value to anyone. Even though the intent of the author may be clear to himself, records are usually meant to be read by others as well. Often the author is not available for an on-the-spot interpretation. The importance of clear wording, good grammar, correct sentence structure, spelling, and proper paragraph structure cannot be overstated. For example, it is imperative that public-service financial records be kept accurately, clearly, and also legibly, since they are subject to audit at any time.

FILING SYSTEMS

Departmental Variances in Filing Needs: Governmental agencies have different departments, each with its various divisions, and often, separate filing systems. For example, the agency's personnel department might have its own filing system, divided into such unique categories as:
- Assignments
- Recruitment
- Training
- Classification
- Separation

Other departments, sections, or divisions would very probably also have filing systems unique to their own needs.

Basic Considerations of Systems: Thus, an effective record keeping system is organized with the programs and functions of the agency kept in mind. The filing system should be as simple as possible, and with accessibility to all clerical workers and members of the professional staff who must use it. A procedure for the periodic removal and disposal or storage of inactive records should be established. One person should be assigned responsibility for the maintenance of the files, with several individuals familiar enough to provide service during emergencies or vacation periods.

Another consideration in establishing a filing system is the security of the storage area from fire and vandalism. For example, school records and draft records have been frequent targets of vandals in recent years.

Filing Procedures: The first step in filing is to separate the materials to be filed from other office materials, inspect them for completeness, and to then determine which type of filing fits the need of that particular project. Some agencies follow a policy of having the responsible party initial the papers, with notes (such as dates) on action completed, and indicating that they are ready for filing. If this is the procedure, filing clerks should first check for the required initials, then read or skim the contents, to assist him when he is later asked to recall important papers. The next step would be to index the material, by mentally classifying it for its method and place of filing.

Manila folders are usually used to protect the papers. It is possible to obtain manila folders in various sizes, but the most common are letter size (8.5 x 11 inches) and legal size (8.5 x 13 inches). After the material has been filed into the cabinet, it is ready for future use.

Each file drawer should have sufficient guides or tabs to lead the eye to the desired section of the file quickly. The guide or tab may be:
- made of the material of the folder
- made of celluloid or other plastic
- made of metal with a plastic window

An angular tab slants back so that a worker does not have to bend over to read captions in lower drawers.

Filing Methods

While much of the detail of modern record keeping is accomplished by computers, there still exists a need for the traditional method of filing certain papers in office files.

Filing Alphabetically: Since this is the case, it is important that all office employees should know at least the basic rules of *alphabetical filing*. Some of the most commonly used filing rules are listed below. With an understanding of these rules, the beginning public-service worker should be able to maintain at least a semblance of order in a filing system:
- File papers by the last name (surname) – Example: Adams before Smith
- When the last names of two or more persons begin with the same first letter, look at the second letter in the names as your aid for selecting the name to be filed in front of the other. If the second letter is the same, then look at the third, and so on. – Example: Jackson before James
- File "nothing" before "something" – Example: Johns before Johnson
- If the last names (surnames) of two or more persons are the same, compare the first letters in the first names to help you decide the order of filing. If the first letters in the first names (given names) are the same, compare the second letters in the given names, and so forth. – Example: "Jones, James" before "Jones, John"
- When a name contains a first name and a middle name or initial, consider the middle name or initial only if the surnames and the given names or initials are alike. – Example: Peters, Anna Mae before Peters, Anna Maria
- The complete name of a person in a business name is considered in the same order as if it appeared by itself. – Example: Thomas, Robert H. Company
- Names of business firms which do not contain complete names of persons are filed according to their first words. If the first words are the same, the second words are considered, and so forth. – Example: J & R Company before Johnson Supply Company
- There are many departments, bureaus, and offices in our Federal Government. When indexing any of these, U.S. Government comes first, followed by the department, bureau, or office.
- State, county, city, and other political subdivisions are indexed under the political subdivision, then under the principal word in the name of the department or office.

Although alphabetical filing is the primary type of filing the beginning public service worker will use, there are other methods of filing with which he should become familiar. These methods include systems for *numeric, subject,* and *geographic* filing:

Filing by the Numeric Method: Numeric filing systems are so called because numbers are used as captions on the guide and folder tabs. Alphabetic systems are direct systems because a person can go directly to the file drawer and, by means of the name captions, file or find records. Numeric systems are indirect because, in most cases, before papers can be placed in or taken from the file drawer, the worker must refer to an alphabetic card index to find the number assigned to a name or subject.

Numeric filing systems can be used to advantage in many circumstances, like:
- where papers would group themselves around definite cases, contracts, or operations that are active for reasonably long but indefinite periods, and that require permanent and extensive cross reference;
- where a file is referred to by number rather than the name of the person involved; or
- in confidential situations where names can be concealed from those handling the files by the use of number captions.

In numeric filing, a number is assigned consecutively to each correspondent or subject that warrants an individual folder as these correspondents or subjects develop. A number once assigned is maintained until a correspondent no longer does business with the agency or company, or a subject ceases to exist. After a specified period, the number may be reassigned. All papers pertaining to the correspondent or subject are placed in the individual folder bearing the number assigned to that correspondent or subject.

A numeric system cannot be operated without a card index that will identify the assigned numbers. Each card contains the name of a correspondent or subject and the number of the folder that has been assigned.

The Social Security system operated by the federal government is based on a numeric filing idea. Schools and colleges have long utilized student numbers, and recently began to use Social Security numbers as the student identification number. Welfare cases have numbers assigned to them and the record keeping is greatly simplified as a result of this means of control. The *Dictionary of Occupational Titles (DOT)* assigns a number to all of the occupations listed.

Filing by Subject: Subject filing is the arrangement of records by names of topics or things rather than by names of people, companies, or locations. Government agencies might find it more convenient to use subject files for these purposes:
- to organize records that do not refer to the name of a person or organization;
- to organize correspondence that is more likely to be called for by its subject than by the name of the correspondent;
- to group records concerning the activities or products of an organization, such as advertising, sales, typewriters, adding machines, etc., so that all the records about one activity or product can be obtained immediately from the files; or
- to group together records that would otherwise fall into very small subdivisions.

Because subject files must meet the requirements of the individual situation, it is unlikely that any two subject files will be organized exactly the same. The nature of the concern would determine the main subject headings, and then subdivisions would be added as necessary.

Filing by Dewey Decimal System: The Dewey Decimal method of classifying information used in libraries, and familiar to most people, is a combination of the subject, numeric, and alphabetical filing systems.

Filing by Geographic Identities: Geographic filing relates to papers arranged in alphabetic order, with sub-listings by location, and then by name or subject. This method has particular advantage for those agencies in which the organization of files or records depends to a large degree on where things happened, or where they are located. As an example, police-department files would probably be organized first on the basis of geographic sections of the city, and then by number, subject, or by the name of the individual concerned in the file.

The specific geographic divisions used will be determined by the filing needs of the agency involved. The primary guides would bear the names of the most important geographic divisions occurring in the operations of the department. The secondary guides would then be used for subdivisions of the main geographic units, as well as for alphabetic sections of the geographic divisions and subdivisions.

MISCELLANEOUS OFFICE RECORDS

Although the type of records and/or the kind of record keeping would vary from office to office, students should be given an introduction to some of the basic records that most office workers would be required to keep, such as petty cash or revolving cash records, budget records, purchase requisitions, purchase orders, and reports.

The book *Clerical Record Keeping* gives a good summary of petty cash records. It provides a thorough study of the various forms that need to be filled out to keep a petty cash fund, and of the affiliated records. It also explains the roles of employees and employers in connection with the records.

The same source book gives a summary of budget records and purchase records. Although designed for the budget records of an individual or a family, the same principles could be utilized in setting up and in maintaining budget records for an office situation. The purchase records go into detail regarding such things as stock record cards, purchase requisition forms, record of goods expected forms, price quotation cards, purchase orders, purchase invoices, and the purchases journal. Although these are slanted toward the needs of a business, they provide an excellent background for understanding the agency's operations outlining its procedures and forms.

The average office worker should also be proficient in knowing how to keep a current and accurate account of the funds in the budget. Various manuals or methods are available which cover very adequately this area of operations.

Many public-service workers find themselves working with payroll records. They must compute the wages from the time shown on time cards, figure gross wages, figure overtime, determine deductions for social security and income tax, and as a result, net pay. The cumulative employee wage records must be kept current, and such forms and reports as withholding tax forms must be prepared at the end of the year.

DATA PROCESSING

Data processing frightens some people. Complicated equipment and procedures that few people can understand are the first things envisioned by the great mass of the population. In its simplest terms, however, data processing is not complicated. Data (which, as you know, is a plural type of word) means unorganized bits of knowledge; processing means to manipulate or to handle. Broadly speaking, therefore, *data processing is the systematizing of many facts into useful organized information.*

A necessary part of the data processing done by a governmental employee is the placing of facts and information into the appropriate order, and recording them in such an organized manner that they can then be readily retrievable or found. The ability to organize and file information has no value if the ability does not also provide for a system to readily find the information, and then to put it to use.

Obtaining and Recording the Data: Every governmental agency, regardless of its size, must process data in order to provide operational information for both the internal needs of management and the external needs of the public. The information provided and the method used to obtain information will vary with the type and size of the agency. The method used will depend upon the volume of data to be processed, the time available for processing the data, and the amount of money that can be spent.

Recording on Forms: Forms are often used to assist in recording data, which facilitates the use of the data in other operations. They are used to communicate data to other individuals or departments; to expedite the storing of data; to increase speed and accuracy in classifying, sorting, and computing data; and to assist in summarizing data so that the information can be easily read. All forms used should be designed to facilitate the processing of data to meet the specific needs of the agency that is using them.

Forms are by no means the only mechanical devices used by record keepers. Those in charge of the handling of forms, and responsible for the information contained on them, have devised and utilized literally hundreds of different methods whereby their work could be done more rapidly and more efficiently.

Mechanical Recorders: Typewriters, imprinting devices, computers, check protectors, time clocks, copying equipment, and duplicating equipment are all means of recording data by the use of mechanical equipment. Various types of calculators (rotary, printing, key-driven, or electronic) are machines that help us to compute data more quickly and accurately. The cash register, that is used almost everywhere goods or services are traded for money, is a mechanism combining the functions of recording, computing, and retrieving essential data.

PROCESSING THE DATA

Electronic-Data Computers: A computer can automatically put data into storage, hold the data there, and then retrieve the data whenever instructed to do so, without human intervention and at electronic speed.

In a computer system, a series of repetitive operations can be performed without human intervention and at high speed. The computer does this by following a series of detailed instructions, called a *program,* which is stored in the computer itself. This stored program tells the computer what data to process, what operations to perform with the data, and what to do with the results; for example, to *store* or *print* the processed information.

Computer Possibilities and Limitations: In addition to doing clerical and accounting work, a computer can also make routine decisions; that is, it can make a choice among alternatives. It can also take alternative courses of action. The computer itself, for example, can select which part of the program to follow, an operation known as *branching.* A computer can also repeat a sequence of instructions; this is known as *looping.*

But, no matter how advanced, or how sophisticated its electronics, a computer can work only with the facts and figures that are fed into it. Obviously then, if wrong information is fed into the computer, wrong results will come out of the machine. Even though the actual computational time is short, the material must be programmed into the machine.

CONTROL SYSTEMS

Surveys of files show that from 1 to 5 percent of records are misfiled, and half of those misfiled are never found. A misfile rate of 1 percent is usually considered normal, but the goal of a government agency is always no misfiled materials. The records of an arrest, a prisoner, or a student's academic record are too important to be lost and, if they should be, the undermining of public confidence in the department would severely weaken its effectiveness.

Even though the greatest possible care has been taken, a paper will occasionally be missing when needed. A few clues, therefore, for conducting systematic searches for missing data may not be inappropriate:

- Look through the folder thoroughly. The paper may have been placed out of order or may be sticking to another paper.
- Look between and under folders. Sometimes a paper is mistakenly placed between folders instead of into the proper folder, and subsequently, is pushed or slips to the bottom of the tray.
- Look under similar names or headings.
- Look for transposed names. A paper may be filed under a first or second name instead of the surname, or it may be filed under the subject's maiden name.
- Check the "out" folders or substitution cards to see who used it last.
- Look in the *To Be Filed, Pending,* or *Suspense* file trays or lists.
- Check for cross-references or related material to see if the paper has been filed there.

If, after a thorough search, the paper is still not located, alert the other workers in your office and make a note to place in the file to prevent someone else from making an extensive search. However, in a well-organized agency, it is seldom that records are lost.

Much time may be saved by establishing and using a control system. If a control system is used, the location of every piece of information is known at all times. There are several major methods of charging out materials, such as these:

- Use of an *out guide;* a stiff guide with the word *out* written on the top. It has a pocket on the front in which may be placed a requisition slip indicating the user, date, and material taken.

- Insertion of an *out folder* in the position of the borrowed folder; this is used to store new material until the regular one is returned.
- Placing of *substitution cards* in regular folder to indicate that material has been removed.

When material has been returned to the files, the out guides, out folders, or substitution cards should be removed from the file. The notations should be crossed out to indicate that the borrower has returned the material.

SUMMARY

Record keeping is an important function of every governmental agency. How it is done will be determined to a large extent by the function of the agency, and the manner in which its records will be used. The manuals published by the agency will usually have detailed instructions covering maintaining of records; however, the people involved need to completely know the procedures, so that time is not wasted consulting the manual every time something is to be filed.

Anyone can stick papers into a file cabinet; however, responsibility does not end there. *The record must be available when needed.* This demands a thorough knowledge of the steps to follow in preparing materials to be filed and the various types of filing and record keeping systems.

LEARNING ACTIVITIES

- Prepare discussion notes on the characteristics of an excellent record keeping system
- Prepare an outline of the various types of classifying information for filing or storage
- Prepare an outline of the rules for alphabetizing material
- Alphabetize the set of index cards prepared by the instructor
- Prepare an outline of the procedures for establishing or using a numerical file
- Each trainee should prepare an organizational or functional chart of the department in which he wishes to work and indicate which records would need to be kept in each of the areas on the chart
- Visit a governmental agency and prepare a report on the record system used. Be sure to note such special problems as classifying and keeping records on fingerprints for future reference.

MANAGEMENT ACTIVITIES

- Prepare a bulletin board illustration of the various types of filing
- Obtain or prepare a set of index cards of the names of individuals, various governmental agencies, and departments which may be used to illustrate filing procedures
- Make a study of the records kept at the local governmental agencies and prepare material for discussion on the why's, how's, and procedures used by the various departments
- Make arrangements to visit a governmental office that utilizes all of the various record keeping devices
- Prepare a discussion on the rules for the alphabetical filing of material
- Obtain the budgetary forms from a governmental office and duplicate some of the simpler forms

- Prepare some simple budgetary problems. Let the class work on them in small groups.
- Prepare a discussion on the rules for the alphabetical filing of material
- Make arrangements with the librarian to demonstrate cross filing
- Encourage the staff to study on their own by reading programmed instruction books on record keeping and data processing
- Arrange for a debate on the advantages and disadvantages of using automated record keeping systems.
- Prepare discussion notes on what to do if some filed matter is lost
- Prepare group activities centered around the problem of keeping inactive files

EVALUATION QUESTIONS

1. Which one is not a basic reason for keeping records?　　　　　　　　　1._____
    A. To prove past actions
    B. To keep the staff working hard
    C. To obtain information for the present
    D. To help in planning for the future

2. Which statement is untrue?　　　　　　　　　2._____
    A. The filing system should be as simple as possible
    B. The filing system should be easily reached by those who use it
    C. Care should be taken that nothing is ever taken out of the filing system
    D. Care should be taken to keep the records storage area safe from fire and vandalism

3. If an agency has collected many papers on one topic or thing, it may use　　3._____
which filing system?
    A. A subject system
    B. A geographic system
    C. A numeric system
    D. The Dewey Decimal System

4. Which type of filing is the Dewey Decimal System based on?　　　　　　4._____
    A. Alphabetical
    B. Subject
    C. Numeric
    D. All of the above

5. The first step in filing is to:　　　　　　　　　5._____
    A. Index the material
    B. Separate the materials from other office material
    C. Inspect them for completeness
    D. Determine which type of filing is best

6. Data processing by public service workers means:
   A. Gathering together unorganized bits of knowledge
   B. Classifying knowledge
   C. Recording knowledge in an organized manner
   D. All of the above

   6._____

7. Which statement is not true about computers?
   A. Information is able to be processed at increasing speeds as computers evolve technologically
   B. A computer can store data and retrieve it when instructed to do so
   C. A computer will not store data that includes wrong information
   D. A computer can do many operations without human beings and at high speed

   7._____

8. If you were looking for a misfiled record it would be wise to:
   A. Look through the folder thoroughly
   B. Check the "out" folders or substitution cards to see who had it last
   C. Look in the "To Be Filed" or "Being Microfilmed" trays
   D. All of the above

   8._____

Answer Key

1. B	4. D	7. C
2. C	5. B	8. D
3. A	6. D	

GLOSSARY OF LEGAL TERMS

TABLE OF CONTENTS

	Page
Action ... Affiant	1
Affidavit ... At Bar	2
At Issue ... Burden of Proof	3
Business ... Commute	4
Complainant ... Conviction	5
Cooperative ... Demur (v.)	6
Demurrage ... Endorsement	7
Enjoin ... Facsimile	8
Factor ... Guilty	9
Habeas Corpus ... Incumbrance	10
Indemnify ... Laches	11
Landlord and Tenant ... Malice	12
Mandamus ... Obiter Dictum	13
Object (v.) ... Perjury	14
Perpetuity ... Proclamation	15
Proffered Evidence ... Referee	16
Referendum ... Stare Decisis	17
State ... Term	18
Testamentary ... Warrant (Warranty) (v.)	19
Warrant (n.) ... Zoning	20

GLOSSARY OF LEGAL TERMS

A

ACTION - "Action" includes a civil action and a criminal action.
A FORTIORI - A term meaning you can reason one thing from the existence of certain facts.
A POSTERIORI - From what goes after; from effect to cause.
A PRIORI - From what goes before; from cause to effect.
AB INITIO - From the beginning.
ABATE - To diminish or put an end to.
ABET - To encourage the commission of a crime.
ABEYANCE - Suspension, temporary suppression.
ABIDE - To accept the consequences of.
ABJURE - To renounce; give up.
ABRIDGE - To reduce; contract; diminish.
ABROGATE - To annul, repeal, or destroy.
ABSCOND - To hide or absent oneself to avoid legal action.
ABSTRACT - A summary.
ABUT - To border on, to touch.
ACCESS - Approach; in real property law it means the right of the owner of property to the use of the highway or road next to his land, without obstruction by intervening property owners.
ACCESSORY - In criminal law, it means the person who contributes or aids in the commission of a crime.
ACCOMMODATED PARTY - One to whom credit is extended on the strength of another person signing a commercial paper.
ACCOMMODATION PAPER - A commercial paper to which the accommodating party has put his name.
ACCOMPLICE - In criminal law, it means a person who together with the principal offender commits a crime.
ACCORD - An agreement to accept something different or less than that to which one is entitled, which extinguishes the entire obligation.
ACCOUNT - A statement of mutual demands in the nature of debt and credit between parties.
ACCRETION - The act of adding to a thing; in real property law, it means gradual accumulation of land by natural causes.
ACCRUE - To grow to; to be added to.
ACKNOWLEDGMENT - The act of going before an official authorized to take acknowledgments, and acknowledging an act as one's own.
ACQUIESCENCE - A silent appearance of consent.
ACQUIT - To legally determine the innocence of one charged with a crime.
AD INFINITUM - Indefinitely.
AD LITEM - For the suit.
AD VALOREM - According to value.
ADJECTIVE LAW - Rules of procedure.
ADJUDICATION - The judgment given in a case.
ADMIRALTY - Court having jurisdiction over maritime cases.
ADULT - Sixteen years old or over (in criminal law).
ADVANCE - In commercial law, it means to pay money or render other value before it is due.
ADVERSE - Opposed; contrary.
ADVOCATE - (v.) To speak in favor of;
              (n.) One who assists, defends, or pleads for another.
AFFIANT - A person who makes and signs an affidavit.

AFFIDAVIT - A written and sworn to declaration of facts, voluntarily made.
AFFINITY- The relationship between persons through marriage with the kindred of each other; distinguished from consanguinity, which is the relationship by blood.
AFFIRM - To ratify; also when an appellate court affirms a judgment, decree, or order, it means that it is valid and right and must stand as rendered in the lower court.
AFOREMENTIONED; AFORESAID - Before or already said.
AGENT - One who represents and acts for another.
AID AND COMFORT - To help; encourage.
ALIAS - A name not one's true name.
ALIBI - A claim of not being present at a certain place at a certain time.
ALLEGE - To assert.
ALLOTMENT - A share or portion.
AMBIGUITY - Uncertainty; capable of being understood in more than one way.
AMENDMENT - Any language made or proposed as a change in some principal writing.
AMICUS CURIAE - A friend of the court; one who has an interest in a case, although not a party in the case, who volunteers advice upon matters of law to the judge. For example, a brief amicus curiae.
AMORTIZATION - To provide for a gradual extinction of (a future obligation) in advance of maturity, especially, by periodical contributions to a sinking fund which will be adequate to discharge a debt or make a replacement when it becomes necessary.
ANCILLARY - Aiding, auxiliary.
ANNOTATION - A note added by way of comment or explanation.
ANSWER - A written statement made by a defendant setting forth the grounds of his defense.
ANTE - Before.
ANTE MORTEM - Before death.
APPEAL - The removal of a case from a lower court to one of superior jurisdiction for the purpose of obtaining a review.
APPEARANCE - Coming into court as a party to a suit.
APPELLANT - The party who takes an appeal from one court or jurisdiction to another (appellate) court for review.
APPELLEE - The party against whom an appeal is taken.
APPROPRIATE - To make a thing one's own.
APPROPRIATION - Prescribing the destination of a thing; the act of the legislature designating a particular fund, to be applied to some object of government expenditure.
APPURTENANT - Belonging to; accessory or incident to.
ARBITER - One who decides a dispute; a referee.
ARBITRARY - Unreasoned; not governed by any fixed rules or standard.
ARGUENDO - By way of argument.
ARRAIGN - To call the prisoner before the court to answer to a charge.
ASSENT - A declaration of willingness to do something in compliance with a request.
ASSERT - Declare.
ASSESS - To fix the rate or amount.
ASSIGN - To transfer; to appoint; to select for a particular purpose.
ASSIGNEE - One who receives an assignment.
ASSIGNOR - One who makes an assignment.
AT BAR - Before the court.

AT ISSUE - When parties in an action come to a point where one asserts something and the other denies it.
ATTACH - Seize property by court order and sometimes arrest a person.
ATTEST - To witness a will, etc.; act of attestation.
AVERMENT - A positive statement of facts.

B

BAIL - To obtain the release of a person from legal custody by giving security and promising that he shall appear in court; to deliver (goods, etc.) in trust to a person for a special purpose.
BAILEE - One to whom personal property is delivered under a contract of bailment.
BAILMENT - Delivery of personal property to another to be held for a certain purpose and to be returned when the purpose is accomplished.
BAILOR - The party who delivers goods to another, under a contract of bailment.
BANC (OR BANK) - Bench; the place where a court sits permanently or regularly; also the assembly of all the judges of a court.
BANKRUPT - An insolvent person, technically, one declared to be bankrupt after a bankruptcy proceeding.
BAR - The legal profession.
BARRATRY - Exciting groundless judicial proceedings.
BARTER - A contract by which parties exchange goods for other goods.
BATTERY - Illegal interfering with another's person.
BEARER - In commercial law, it means the person in possession of a commercial paper which is payable to the bearer.
BENCH - The court itself or the judge.
BENEFICIARY - A person benefiting under a will, trust, or agreement.
BEST EVIDENCE RULE, THE - Except as otherwise provided by statute, no evidence other than the writing itself is admissible to prove the content of a writing. This section shall be known and may be cited as the best evidence rule.
BEQUEST - A gift of personal property under a will.
BILL - A formal written statement of complaint to a court of justice; also, a draft of an act of the legislature before it becomes a law; also, accounts for goods sold, services rendered, or work done.
BONA FIDE - In or with good faith; honestly.
BOND - An instrument by which the maker promises to pay a sum of money to another, usually providing that upon performances of a certain condition the obligation shall be void.
BOYCOTT - A plan to prevent the carrying on of a business by wrongful means.
BREACH - The breaking or violating of a law, or the failure to carry out a duty.
BRIEF - A written document, prepared by a lawyer to serve as the basis of an argument upon a case in court, usually an appellate court.
BURDEN OF PRODUCING EVIDENCE - The obligation of a party to introduce evidence sufficient to avoid a ruling against him on the issue.
BURDEN OF PROOF - The obligation of a party to establish by evidence a requisite degree of belief concerning a fact in the mind of the trier of fact or the court. The burden of proof may require a party to raise a reasonable doubt concerning the existence of nonexistence of a fact or that he establish the existence or nonexistence of a fact by a preponderance of the evidence, by clear and convincing proof, or by proof beyond a reasonable doubt.
   Except as otherwise provided by law, the burden of proof requires proof by a preponderance of the evidence.

BUSINESS, A - Shall include every kind of business, profession, occupation, calling or operation of institutions, whether carried on for profit or not.

BY-LAWS - Regulations, ordinances, or rules enacted by a corporation, association, etc., for its own government.

C

CANON - A doctrine; also, a law or rule, of a church or association in particular.

CAPIAS - An order to arrest.

CAPTION - In a pleading, deposition or other paper connected with a case in court, it is the heading or introductory clause which shows the names of the parties, name of the court, number of the case on the docket or calendar, etc.

CARRIER - A person or corporation undertaking to transport persons or property.

CASE - A general term for an action, cause, suit, or controversy before a judicial body.

CAUSE - A suit, litigation or action before a court.

CAVEAT EMPTOR - Let the buyer beware. This term expresses the rule that the purchaser of an article must examine, judge, and test it for himself, being bound to discover any obvious defects or imperfections.

CERTIFICATE - A written representation that some legal formality has been complied with.

CERTIORARI - To be informed of; the name of a writ issued by a superior court directing the lower court to send up to the former the record and proceedings of a case.

CHANGE OF VENUE - To remove place of trial from one place to another.

CHARGE - An obligation or duty; a formal complaint; an instruction of the court to the jury upon a case.

CHARTER - (n.) The authority by virtue of which an organized body acts;
 (v.) in mercantile law, it means to hire or lease a vehicle or vessel for transportation.

CHATTEL - An article of personal property.

CHATTEL MORTGAGE - A mortgage on personal property.

CIRCUIT - A division of the country, for the administration of justice; a geographical area served by a court.

CITATION - The act of the court by which a person is summoned or cited; also, a reference to legal authority.

CIVIL (ACTIONS)- It indicates the private rights and remedies of individuals in contrast to the word "criminal" (actions) which relates to prosecution for violation of laws.

CLAIM (n.) - Any demand held or asserted as of right.

CODICIL - An addition to a will.

CODIFY - To arrange the laws of a country into a code.

COGNIZANCE - Notice or knowledge.

COLLATERAL - By the side; accompanying; an article or thing given to secure performance of a promise.

COMITY - Courtesy; the practice by which one court follows the decision of another court on the same question.

COMMIT - To perform, as an act; to perpetrate, as a crime; to send a person to prison.

COMMON LAW - As distinguished from law created by the enactment of the legislature (called statutory law), it relates to those principles and rules of action which derive their authority solely from usages and customs of immemorial antiquity, particularly with reference to the ancient unwritten law of England. The written pronouncements of the common law are found in court decisions.

COMMUTE - Change punishment to one less severe.

COMPLAINANT - One who applies to the court for legal redress.
COMPLAINT - The pleading of a plaintiff in a civil action; or a charge that a person has committed a specified offense.
COMPROMISE - An arrangement for settling a dispute by agreement.
CONCUR - To agree, consent.
CONCURRENT - Running together, at the same time.
CONDEMNATION - Taking private property for public use on payment therefor.
CONDITION - Mode or state of being; a qualification or restriction.
CONDUCT - Active and passive behavior; both verbal and nonverbal.
CONFESSION - Voluntary statement of guilt of crime.
CONFIDENTIAL COMMUNICATION BETWEEN CLIENT AND LAWYER - Information transmitted between a client and his lawyer in the course of that relationship and in confidence by a means which, so far as the client is aware, discloses the information to no third persons other than those who are present to further the interest of the client in the consultation or those to whom disclosure is reasonably necessary for the transmission of the information or the accomplishment of the purpose for which the lawyer is consulted, and includes a legal opinion formed and the advice given by the lawyer in the course of that relationship.
CONFRONTATION - Witness testifying in presence of defendant.
CONSANGUINITY - Blood relationship.
CONSIGN - To give in charge; commit; entrust; to send or transmit goods to a merchant, factor, or agent for sale.
CONSIGNEE - One to whom a consignment is made.
CONSIGNOR - One who sends or makes a consignment.
CONSPIRACY - In criminal law, it means an agreement between two or more persons to commit an unlawful act.
CONSPIRATORS - Persons involved in a conspiracy.
CONSTITUTION - The fundamental law of a nation or state.
CONSTRUCTION OF GENDERS - The masculine gender includes the feminine and neuter.
CONSTRUCTION OF SINGULAR AND PLURAL - The singular number includes the plural; and the plural, the singular.
CONSTRUCTION OF TENSES - The present tense includes the past and future tenses; and the future, the present.
CONSTRUCTIVE - An act or condition assumed from other parts or conditions.
CONSTRUE - To ascertain the meaning of language.
CONSUMMATE - To complete.
CONTIGUOUS - Adjoining; touching; bounded by.
CONTINGENT - Possible, but not assured; dependent upon some condition.
CONTINUANCE - The adjournment or postponement of an action pending in a court.
CONTRA - Against, opposed to; contrary.
CONTRACT - An agreement between two or more persons to do or not to do a particular thing.
CONTROVERT - To dispute, deny.
CONVERSION - Dealing with the personal property of another as if it were one's own, without right.
CONVEYANCE - An instrument transferring title to land.
CONVICTION - Generally, the result of a criminal trial which ends in a judgment or sentence that the defendant is guilty as charged.

COOPERATIVE - A cooperative is a voluntary organization of persons with a common interest, formed and operated along democratic lines for the purpose of supplying services at cost to its members and other patrons, who contribute both capital and business.
CORPUS DELICTI - The body of a crime; the crime itself.
CORROBORATE - To strengthen; to add weight by additional evidence.
COUNTERCLAIM - A claim presented by a defendant in opposition to or deduction from the claim of the plaintiff.
COUNTY - Political subdivision of a state.
COVENANT - Agreement.
CREDIBLE - Worthy of belief.
CREDITOR - A person to whom a debt is owing by another person, called the "debtor."
CRIMINAL ACTION - Includes criminal proceedings.
CRIMINAL INFORMATION - Same as complaint.
CRITERION (sing.)
CRITERIA (plural) - A means or tests for judging; a standard or standards.
CROSS-EXAMINATION - Examination of a witness by a party other than the direct examiner upon a matter that is within the scope of the direct examination of the witness.
CULPABLE - Blamable.
CY-PRES - As near as (possible). The rule of *cy-pres* is a rule for the construction of instruments in equity by which the intention of the party is carried out *as near as may be*, when it would be impossible or illegal to give it literal effect.

D

DAMAGES - A monetary compensation, which may be recovered in the courts by any person who has suffered loss, or injury, whether to his person, property or rights through the unlawful act or omission or negligence of another.
DECLARANT - A person who makes a statement.
DE FACTO - In fact; actually but without legal authority.
DE JURE - Of right; legitimate; lawful.
DE MINIMIS - Very small or trifling.
DE NOVO - Anew; afresh; a second time.
DEBT - A specified sum of money owing to one person from another, including not only the obligation of the debtor to pay, but the right of the creditor to receive and enforce payment.
DECEDENT - A dead person.
DECISION - A judgment or decree pronounced by a court in determination of a case.
DECREE - An order of the court, determining the rights of all parties to a suit.
DEED - A writing containing a contract sealed and delivered; particularly to convey real property.
DEFALCATION - Misappropriation of funds.
DEFAMATION - Injuring one's reputation by false statements.
DEFAULT - The failure to fulfill a duty, observe a promise, discharge an obligation, or perform an agreement.
DEFENDANT - The person defending or denying; the party against whom relief or recovery is sought in an action or suit.
DEFRAUD - To practice fraud; to cheat or trick.
DELEGATE (v.)- To entrust to the care or management of another.
DELICTUS - A crime.
DEMUR (v.) - To dispute the sufficiency in law of the pleading of the other side.

DEMURRAGE - In maritime law, it means, the sum fixed or allowed as remuneration to the owners of a ship for the detention of their vessel beyond the number of days allowed for loading and unloading or for sailing; also used in railroad terminology.
DENIAL - A form of pleading; refusing to admit the truth of a statement, charge, etc.
DEPONENT - One who gives testimony under oath reduced to writing.
DEPOSITION - Testimony given under oath outside of court for use in court or for the purpose of obtaining information in preparation for trial of a case.
DETERIORATION - A degeneration such as from decay, corrosion or disintegration.
DETRIMENT - Any loss or harm to person or property.
DEVIATION - A turning aside.
DEVISE - A gift of real property by the last will and testament of the donor.
DICTUM (sing.)
DICTA (plural) - Any statements made by the court in an opinion concerning some rule of law not necessarily involved nor essential to the determination of the case.
DIRECT EVIDENCE - Evidence that directly proves a fact, without an inference or presumption, and which in itself if true, conclusively establishes that fact.
DIRECT EXAMINATION - The first examination of a witness upon a matter that is not within the scope of a previous examination of the witness.
DISAFFIRM - To repudiate.
DISMISS - In an action or suit, it means to dispose of the case without any further consideration or hearing.
DISSENT - To denote disagreement of one or more judges of a court with the decision passed by the majority upon a case before them.
DOCKET (n.) - A formal record, entered in brief, of the proceedings in a court.
DOCTRINE - A rule, principle, theory of law.
DOMICILE - That place where a man has his true, fixed and permanent home to which whenever he is absent he has the intention of returning.
DRAFT (n.) - A commercial paper ordering payment of money drawn by one person on another.
DRAWEE - The person who is requested to pay the money.
DRAWER - The person who draws the commercial paper and addresses it to the drawee.
DUPLICATE - A counterpart produced by the same impression as the original enlargements and miniatures, or by mechanical or electronic re-recording, or by chemical reproduction, or by other equivalent technique which accurately reproduces the original.
DURESS - Use of force to compel performance or non-performance of an act.

E

EASEMENT - A liberty, privilege, or advantage without profit, in the lands of another.
EGRESS - Act or right of going out or leaving; emergence.
EIUSDEM GENERIS - Of the same kind, class or nature. A rule used in the construction of language in a legal document.
EMBEZZLEMENT - To steal; to appropriate fraudulently to one's own use property entrusted to one's care.
EMBRACERY - Unlawful attempt to influence jurors, etc., but not by offering value.
EMINENT DOMAIN - The right of a state to take private property for public use.
ENACT - To make into a law.
ENDORSEMENT - Act of writing one's name on the back of a note, bill or similar written instrument.

ENJOIN - To require a person, by writ of injunction from a court of equity, to perform or to abstain or desist from some act.
ENTIRETY - The whole; that which the law considers as one whole, and not capable of being divided into parts.
ENTRAPMENT - Inducing one to commit a crime so as to arrest him.
ENUMERATED - Mentioned specifically; designated.
ENURE - To operate or take effect.
EQUITY - In its broadest sense, this term denotes the spirit and the habit of fairness, justness, and right dealing which regulate the conduct of men.
ERROR - A mistake of law, or the false or irregular application of law as will nullify the judicial proceedings.
ESCROW - A deed, bond or other written engagement, delivered to a third person, to be delivered by him only upon the performance or fulfillment of some condition.
ESTATE - The interest which any one has in lands, or in any other subject of property.
ESTOP - To stop, bar, or impede.
ESTOPPEL - A rule of law which prevents a man from alleging or denying a fact, because of his own previous act.
ET AL. (alii) - And others.
ET SEQ. (sequential) - And the following.
ET UX. (uxor) - And wife.
EVIDENCE - Testimony, writings, material objects, or other things presented to the senses that are offered to prove the existence or non-existence of a fact.
    Means from which inferences may be drawn as a basis of proof in duly constituted judicial or fact finding tribunals, and includes testimony in the form of opinion and hearsay.
EX CONTRACTU
EX DELICTO - In law, rights and causes of action are divided into two classes, those arising *ex contractu* (from a contract) and those arising *ex delicto* (from a delict or tort).
EX OFFICIO - From office; by virtue of the office.
EX PARTE - On one side only; by or for one.
EX POST FACTO - After the fact.
EX POST FACTO LAW - A law passed after an act was done which retroactively makes such act a crime.
EX REL. (relations) - Upon relation or information.
EXCEPTION - An objection upon a matter of law to a decision made, either before or after judgment by a court.
EXECUTOR (male)
EXECUTRIX (female) - A person who has been appointed by will to execute the will.
EXECUTORY - That which is yet to be executed or performed.
EXEMPT - To release from some liability to which others are subject.
EXONERATION - The removal of a burden, charge or duty.
EXTRADITION - Surrender of a fugitive from one nation to another.

F

F.A.S.- "Free alongside ship"; delivery at dock for ship named.
F.O.B.- "Free on board"; seller will deliver to car, truck, vessel, or other conveyance by which goods are to be transported, without expense or risk of loss to the buyer or consignee.
FABRICATE - To construct; to invent a false story.
FACSIMILE - An exact or accurate copy of an original instrument.

FACTOR - A commercial agent.
FEASANCE - The doing of an act.
FELONIOUS - Criminal, malicious.
FELONY - Generally, a criminal offense that may be punished by death or imprisonment for more than one year as differentiated from a misdemeanor.
FEME SOLE - A single woman.
FIDUCIARY - A person who is invested with rights and powers to be exercised for the benefit of another person.
FIERI FACIAS - A writ of execution commanding the sheriff to levy and collect the amount of a judgment from the goods and chattels of the judgment debtor.
FINDING OF FACT - Determination from proof or judicial notice of the existence of a fact. A ruling implies a supporting finding of fact; no separate or formal finding is required unless required by a statute of this state.
FISCAL - Relating to accounts or the management of revenue.
FORECLOSURE (sale) - A sale of mortgaged property to obtain satisfaction of the mortgage out of the sale proceeds.
FORFEITURE - A penalty, a fine.
FORGERY - Fabricating or producing falsely, counterfeited.
FORTUITOUS - Accidental.
FORUM - A court of justice; a place of jurisdiction.
FRAUD - Deception; trickery.
FREEHOLDER - One who owns real property.
FUNGIBLE - Of such kind or nature that one specimen or part may be used in the place of another.

G

GARNISHEE - Person garnished.
GARNISHMENT - A legal process to reach the money or effects of a defendant, in the possession or control of a third person.
GRAND JURY - Not less than 16, not more than 23 citizens of a county sworn to inquire into crimes committed or triable in the county.
GRANT - To agree to; convey, especially real property.
GRANTEE - The person to whom a grant is made.
GRANTOR - The person by whom a grant is made.
GRATUITOUS - Given without a return, compensation or consideration.
GRAVAMEN - The grievance complained of or the substantial cause of a criminal action.
GUARANTY (n.) - A promise to answer for the payment of some debt, or the performance of some duty, in case of the failure of another person, who, in the first instance, is liable for such payment or performance.
GUARDIAN - The person, committee, or other representative authorized by law to protect the person or estate or both of an incompetent (or of a *sui juris* person having a guardian) and to act for him in matters affecting his person or property or both. An incompetent is a person under disability imposed by law.
GUILTY - Establishment of the fact that one has committed a breach of conduct; especially, a violation of law.

H

HABEAS CORPUS - You have the body; the name given to a variety of writs, having for their object to bring a party before a court or judge for decision as to whether such person is being lawfully held prisoner.
HABENDUM - In conveyancing; it is the clause in a deed conveying land which defines the extent of ownership to be held by the grantee.
HEARING - A proceeding whereby the arguments of the interested parties are heared.
HEARSAY - A type of testimony given by a witness who relates, not what he knows personally, but what others have told hi, or what he has heard said by others.
HEARSAY RULE, THE - (a) "Hearsay evidence" is evidence of a statement that was made other than by a witness while testifying at the hearing and that is offered to prove the truth of the matter stated; (b) Except as provided by law, hearsay evidence is inadmissible; (c) This section shall be known and may be cited as the hearsay rule.
HEIR - Generally, one who inherits property, real or personal.
HOLDER OF THE PRIVILEGE - (a) The client when he has no guardian or conservator; (b) A guardian or conservator of the client when the client has a guardian or conservator; (c) The personal representative of the client if the client is dead; (d) A successor, assign, trustee in dissolution, or any similar representative of a firm, association, organization, partnership, business trust, corporation, or public entity that is no longer in existence.
HUNG JURY - One so divided that they can't agree on a verdict.
HUSBAND-WIFE PRIVILEGE - An accused in a criminal proceeding has a privilege to prevent his spouse from testifying against him.
HYPOTHECATE - To pledge a thing without delivering it to the pledgee.
HYPOTHESIS - A supposition, assumption, or toehry.

I

I.E. (id est) - That is.
IB., OR IBID.(ibidem) - In the same place; used to refer to a legal reference previously cited to avoid repeating the entire citation.
ILLICIT - Prohibited; unlawful.
ILLUSORY - Deceiving by false appearance.
IMMUNITY - Exemption.
IMPEACH - To accuse, to dispute.
IMPEDIMENTS - Disabilities, or hindrances.
IMPLEAD - To sue or prosecute by due course of law.
IMPUTED - Attributed or charged to.
IN LOCO PARENTIS - In place of parent, a guardian.
IN TOTO - In the whole; completely.
INCHOATE - Imperfect; unfinished.
INCOMMUNICADO - Denial of the right of a prisoner to communicate with friends or relatives.
INCOMPETENT - One who is incapable of caring for his own affairs because he is mentally deficient or undeveloped.
INCRIMINATION - A matter will incriminate a person if it constitutes, or forms an essential part of, or, taken in connection with other matters disclosed, is a basis for a reasonable inference of such a violation of the laws of this State as to subject him to liability to punishment therefor, unless he has become for any reason permanently immune from punishment for such violation.
INCUMBRANCE - Generally a claim, lien, charge or liability attached to and binding real property.

INDEMNIFY - To secure against loss or damage; also, to make reimbursement to one for a loss already incurred by him.

INDEMNITY - An agreement to reimburse another person in case of an anticipated loss falling upon him.

INDICIA - Signs; indications.

INDICTMENT - An accusation in writing found and presented by a grand jury charging that a person has committed a crime.

INDORSE - To write a name on the back of a legal paper or document, generally, a negotiable instrument

INDUCEMENT - Cause or reason why a thing is done or that which incites the person to do the act or commit a crime; the motive for the criminal act.

INFANT - In civil cases one under 21 years of age.

INFORMATION - A formal accusation of crime made by a prosecuting attorney.

INFRA - Below, under; this word occurring by itself in a publication refers the reader to a future part of the publication.

INGRESS - The act of going into.

INJUNCTION - A writ or order by the court requiring a person, generally, to do or to refrain from doing an act.

INSOLVENT - The condition of a person who is unable to pay his debts.

INSTRUCTION - A direction given by the judge to the jury concerning the law of the case.

INTERIM - In the meantime; time intervening.

INTERLOCUTORY - Temporary, not final; something intervening between the commencement and the end of a suit which decides some point or matter, but is not a final decision of the whole controversy.

INTERROGATORIES - A series of formal written questions used in the examination of a party or a witness usually prior to a trial.

INTESTATE - A person who dies without a will.

INURE - To result, to take effect.

IPSO FACTO - By the fact iself; by the mere fact.

ISSUE (n.) The disputed point or question in a case,

J

JEOPARDY - Danger, hazard, peril.

JOINDER - Joining; uniting with another person in some legal steps or proceeding.

JOINT - United; combined.

JUDGE - Member or members or representative or representatives of a court conducting a trial or hearing at which evidence is introduced.

JUDGMENT - The official decision of a court of justice.

JUDICIAL OR JUDICIARY - Relating to or connected with the administration of justice.

JURAT - The clause written at the foot of an affidavit, stating when, where and before whom such affidavit was sworn.

JURISDICTION - The authority to hear and determine controversies between parties.

JURISPRUDENCE - The philosophy of law.

JURY - A body of persons legally selected to inquire into any matter of fact, and to render their verdict according to the evidence.

L

LACHES - The failure to diligently assert a right, which results in a refusal to allow relief.

LANDLORD AND TENANT - A phrase used to denote the legal relation existing between the owner and occupant of real estate.

LARCENY - Stealing personal property belonging to another.

LATENT - Hidden; that which does not appear on the face of a thing.

LAW - Includes constitutional, statutory, and decisional law.

LAWYER-CLIENT PRIVILEGE - (1) A "client" is a person, public officer, or corporation, association, or other organization or entity, either public or private, who is rendered professional legal services by a lawyer, or who consults a lawyer with a view to obtaining professional legal services from him; (2) A "lawyer" is a person authorized, or reasonably believed by the client to be authorized, to practice law in any state or nation; (3) A "representative of the lawyer" is one employed to assist the lawyer in the rendition of professional legal services; (4) A communication is "confidential" if not intended to be disclosed to third persons other than those to whom disclosure is in furtherance of the rendition of professional legal services to the client or those reasonably necessary for the transmission of the communication.

General rule of privilege - A client has a privilege to refuse to disclose and to prevent any other person from disclosing confidential communications made for the purpose of facilitating the rendition of professional legal services to the client, (1) between himself or his representative and his lawyer or his lawyer's representative, or (2) between his lawyer and the lawyer's representative, or (3) by him or his lawyer to a lawyer representing another in a matter of common interest, or (4) between representatives of the client or between the client and a representative of the client, or (5) between lawyers representing the client.

LEADING QUESTION - Question that suggests to the witness the answer that the examining party desires.

LEASE - A contract by which one conveys real estate for a limited time usually for a specified rent; personal property also may be leased.

LEGISLATION - The act of enacting laws.

LEGITIMATE - Lawful.

LESSEE - One to whom a lease is given.

LESSOR - One who grants a lease

LEVY - A collecting or exacting by authority.

LIABLE - Responsible; bound or obligated in law or equity.

LIBEL (v.) - To defame or injure a person's reputation by a published writing.

(n.) - The initial pleading on the part of the plaintiff in an admiralty proceeding.

LIEN - A hold or claim which one person has upon the property of another as a security for some debt or charge.

LIQUIDATED - Fixed; settled.

LIS PENDENS - A pending civil or criminal action.

LITERAL - According to the language.

LITIGANT - A party to a lawsuit.

LITATION - A judicial controversy.

LOCUS - A place.

LOCUS DELICTI - Place of the crime.

LOCUS POENITENTIAE - The abandoning or giving up of one's intention to commit some crime before it is fully completed or abandoning a conspiracy before its purpose is accomplished.

M

MALFEASANCE - To do a wrongful act.

MALICE - The doing of a wrongful act Intentionally without just cause or excuse.

MANDAMUS - The name of a writ issued by a court to enforce the performance of some public duty.
MANDATORY (adj.) Containing a command.
MARITIME - Pertaining to the sea or to commerce thereon.
MARSHALING - Arranging or disposing of in order.
MAXIM - An established principle or proposition.
MINISTERIAL - That which involves obedience to instruction, but demands no special discretion, judgment or skill.
MISAPPROPRIATE - Dealing fraudulently with property entrusted to one.
MISDEMEANOR - A crime less than a felony and punishable by a fine or imprisonment for less than one year.
MISFEASANCE - Improper performance of a lawful act.
MISREPRESENTATION - An untrue representation of facts.
MITIGATE - To make or become less severe, harsh.
MITTIMUS - A warrant of commitment to prison.
MOOT (adj.) Unsettled, undecided, not necessary to be decided.
MORTGAGE - A conveyance of property upon condition, as security for the payment of a debt or the performance of a duty, and to become void upon payment or performance according to the stipulated terms.
MORTGAGEE - A person to whom property is mortgaged.
MORTGAGOR - One who gives a mortgage.
MOTION - In legal proceedings, a "motion" is an application, either written or oral, addressed to the court by a party to an action or a suit requesting the ruling of the court on a matter of law.
MUTUALITY - Reciprocation.

N

NEGLIGENCE - The failure to exercise that degree of care which an ordinarily prudent person would exercise under like circumstances.
NEGOTIABLE (instrument) - Any instrument obligating the payment of money which is transferable from one person to another by endorsement and delivery or by delivery only.
NEGOTIATE - To transact business; to transfer a negotiable instrument; to seek agreement for the amicable disposition of a controversy or case.
NOLLE PROSEQUI - A formal entry upon the record, by the plaintiff in a civil suit or the prosecuting officer in a criminal action, by which he declares that he "will no further prosecute" the case.
NOLO CONTENDERE - The name of a plea in a criminal action, having the same effect as a plea of guilty; but not constituting a direct admission of guilt.
NOMINAL - Not real or substantial.
NOMINAL DAMAGES - Award of a trifling sum where no substantial injury is proved to have been sustained.
NONFEASANCE - Neglect of duty.
NOVATION - The substitution of a new debt or obligation for an existing one.
NUNC PRO TUNC - A phrase applied to acts allowed to be done after the time when they should be done, with a retroactive effect.("Now for then.")

O

OATH - Oath includes affirmation or declaration under penalty of perjury.
OBITER DICTUM - Opinion expressed by a court on a matter not essentially involved in a case and hence not a decision; also called dicta, if plural.

OBJECT (v.) - To oppose as improper or illegal and referring the question of its propriety or legality to the court.
OBLIGATION - A legal duty, by which a person is bound to do or not to do a certain thing.
OBLIGEE - The person to whom an obligation is owed.
OBLIGOR - The person who is to perform the obligation.
OFFER (v.) - To present for acceptance or rejection.
    (n.) - A proposal to do a thing, usually a proposal to make a contract.
OFFICIAL INFORMATION - Information within the custody or control of a department or agency of the government the disclosure of which is shown to be contrary to the public interest.
OFFSET - A deduction.
ONUS PROBANDI - Burden of proof.
OPINION - The statement by a judge of the decision reached in a case, giving the law as applied to the case and giving reasons for the judgment; also a belief or view.
OPTION - The exercise of the power of choice; also a privilege existing in one person, for which he has paid money, which gives him the right to buy or sell real or personal property at a given price within a specified time.
ORDER - A rule or regulation; every direction of a court or judge made or entered in writing but not including a judgment.
ORDINANCE - Generally, a rule established by authority; also commonly used to designate the legislative acts of a municipal corporation.
ORIGINAL - Writing or recording itself or any counterpart intended to have the same effect by a person executing or issuing it. An "original" of a photograph includes the negative or any print therefrom. If data are stored in a computer or similar device, any printout or other output readable by sight, shown to reflect the data accurately, is an "original."
OVERT - Open, manifest.

P

PANEL - A group of jurors selected to serve during a term of the court.
PARENS PATRIAE - Sovereign power of a state to protect or be a guardian over children and incompetents.
PAROL - Oral or verbal.
PAROLE - To release one in prison before the expiration of his sentence, conditionally.
PARITY - Equality in purchasing power between the farmer and other segments of the economy.
PARTITION - A legal division of real or personal property between one or more owners.
PARTNERSHIP - An association of two or more persons to carry on as co-owners a business for profit.
PATENT (adj.) - Evident.
    (n.) - A grant of some privilege, property, or authority, made by the government or sovereign of a country to one or more individuals.
PECULATION - Stealing.
PECUNIARY - Monetary.
PENULTIMATE - Next to the last.
PER CURIAM - A phrase used in the report of a decision to distinguish an opinion of the whole court from an opinion written by any one judge.
PER SE - In itself; taken alone.
PERCEIVE - To acquire knowledge through one's senses.
PEREMPTORY - Imperative; absolute.
PERJURY - To lie or state falsely under oath.

PERPETUITY - Perpetual existence; also the quality or condition of an estate limited so that it will not take effect or vest within the period fixed by law.
PERSON - Includes a natural person, firm, association, organization, partnership, business trust, corporation, or public entity.
PERSONAL PROPERTY - Includes money, goods, chattels, things in action, and evidences of debt.
PERSONALTY - Short term for personal property.
PETITION - An application in writing for an order of the court, stating the circumstances upon which it is founded and requesting any order or other relief from a court.
PLAINTIFF - A person who brings a court action.
PLEA - A pleading in a suit or action.
PLEADINGS - Formal allegations made by the parties of their respective claims and defenses, for the judgment of the court.
PLEDGE - A deposit of personal property as a security for the performance of an act.
PLEDGEE - The party to whom goods are delivered in pledge.
PLEDGOR - The party delivering goods in pledge.
PLENARY - Full; complete.
POLICE POWER - Inherent power of the state or its political subdivisions to enact laws within constitutional limits to promote the general welfare of society or the community.
POLLING THE JURY - Call the names of persons on a jury and requiring each juror to declare what his verdict is before it is legally recorded.
POST MORTEM - After death.
POWER OF ATTORNEY - A writing authorizing one to act for another.
PRECEPT - An order, warrant, or writ issued to an officer or body of officers, commanding him or them to do some act within the scope of his or their powers.
PRELIMINARY FACT - Fact upon the existence or nonexistence of which depends the admissibility or inadmissibility of evidence. The phrase "the admissibility or inadmissibility of evidence" includes the qualification or disqualification of a person to be a witness and the existence or nonexistence of a privilege.
PREPONDERANCE - Outweighing.
PRESENTMENT - A report by a grand jury on something they have investigated on their own knowledge.
PRESUMPTION - An assumption of fact resulting from a rule of law which requires such fact to be assumed from another fact or group of facts found or otherwise established in the action.
PRIMA FACUE - At first sight.
PRIMA FACIE CASE - A case where the evidence is very patent against the defendant.
PRINCIPAL - The source of authority or rights; a person primarily liable as differentiated from "principle" as a primary or basic doctrine.
PRO AND CON - For and against.
PRO RATA - Proportionally.
PROBATE - Relating to proof, especially to the proof of wills.
PROBATIVE - Tending to prove.
PROCEDURE - In law, this term generally denotes rules which are established by the Federal, State, or local Governments regarding the types of pleading and courtroom practice which must be followed by the parties involved in a criminal or civil case.
PROCLAMATION - A public notice by an official of some order, intended action, or state of facts.

PROFFERED EVIDENCE - The admissibility or inadmissibility of which is dependent upon the existence or nonexistence of a preliminary fact.
PROMISSORY (NOTE) - A promise in writing to pay a specified sum at an expressed time, or on demand, or at sight, to a named person, or to his order, or bearer.
PROOF - The establishment by evidence of a requisite degree of belief concerning a fact in the mind of the trier of fact or the court.
PROPERTY - Includes both real and personal property.
PROPRIETARY (adj.) - Relating or pertaining to ownership; usually a single owner.
PROSECUTE - To carry on an action or other judicial proceeding; to proceed against a person criminally.
PROVISO - A limitation or condition in a legal instrument.
PROXIMATE - Immediate; nearest
PUBLIC EMPLOYEE - An officer, agent, or employee of a public entity.
PUBLIC ENTITY - Includes a national, state, county, city and county, city, district, public authority, public agency, or any other political subdivision or public corporation, whether foreign or domestic.
PUBLIC OFFICIAL - Includes an official of a political dubdivision of such state or territory and of a municipality.
PUNITIVE - Relating to punishment.

Q

QUASH - To make void.
QUASI - As if; as it were.
QUID PRO QUO - Something for something; the giving of one valuable thing for another.
QUITCLAIM (v.) - To release or relinquish claim or title to, especially in deeds to realty.
QUO WARRANTO - A legal procedure to test an official's right to a public office or the right to hold a franchise, or to hold an office in a domestic corporation.

R

RATIFY - To approve and sanction.
REAL PROPERTY - Includes lands, tenements, and hereditaments.
REALTY - A brief term for real property.
REBUT - To contradict; to refute, especially by evidence and arguments.
RECEIVER - A person who is appointed by the court to receive, and hold in trust property in litigation.
RECIDIVIST - Habitual criminal.
RECIPROCAL - Mutual.
RECOUPMENT - To keep back or get something which is due; also, it is the right of a defendant to have a deduction from the amount of the plaintiff's damages because the plaintiff has not fulfilled his part of the same contract.
RECROSS EXAMINATION - Examination of a witness by a cross-examiner subsequent to a redirect examination of the witness.
REDEEM - To release an estate or article from mortgage or pledge by paying the debt for which it stood as security.
REDIRECT EXAMINATION - Examination of a witness by the direct examiner subsequent to the cross-examination of the witness.
REFEREE - A person to whom a cause pending in a court is referred by the court, to take testimony, hear the parties, and report thereon to the court.

REFERENDUM - A method of submitting an important legislative or administrative matter to a direct vote of the people.
RELEVANT EVIDENCE - Evidence including evidence relevant to the credulity of a witness or hearsay declarant, having any tendency in reason to prove or disprove any disputed fact that is of consequence to the determination of the action.
REMAND - To send a case back to the lower court from which it came, for further proceedings.
REPLEVIN - An action to recover goods or chattels wrongfully taken or detained.
REPLY (REPLICATION) - Generally, a reply is what the plaintiff or other person who has instituted proceedings says in answer to the defendant's case.
RE JUDICATA - A thing judicially acted upon or decided.
RES ADJUDICATA - Doctrine that an issue or dispute litigated and determined in a case between the opposing parties is deemed permanently decided between these parties.
RESCIND (RECISSION) - To avoid or cancel a contract.
RESPONDENT - A defendant in a proceeding in chancery or admiralty; also, the person who contends against the appeal in a case.
RESTITUTION - In equity, it is the restoration of both parties to their original condition (when practicable), upon the rescission of a contract for fraud or similar cause.
RETROACTIVE (RETROSPECTIVE) - Looking back; effective as of a prior time.
REVERSED - A term used by appellate courts to indicate that the decision of the lower court in the case before it has been set aside.
REVOKE - To recall or cancel.
RIPARIAN (RIGHTS) - The rights of a person owning land containing or bordering on a water course or other body of water, such as lakes and rivers.

S

SALE - A contract whereby the ownership of property is transferred from one person to another for a sum of money or for any consideration.
SANCTION - A penalty or punishment provided as a means of enforcing obedience to a law; also, an authorization.
SATISFACTION - The discharge of an obligation by paying a party what is due to him; or what is awarded to him by the judgment of a court or otherwise.
SCIENTER - Knowingly; also, it is used in pleading to denote the defendant's guilty knowledge.
SCINTILLA - A spark; also the least particle.
SECRET OF STATE - Governmental secret relating to the national defense or the international relations of the United States.
SECURITY - Indemnification; the term is applied to an obligation, such as a mortgage or deed of trust, given by a debtor to insure the payment or performance of his debt, by furnishing the creditor with a resource to be used in case of the debtor's failure to fulfill the principal obligation.
SENTENCE - The judgment formally pronounced by the court or judge upon the defendant after his conviction in a criminal prosecution.
SET-OFF - A claim or demand which one party in an action credits against the claim of the opposing party.
SHALL and MAY - "Shall" is mandatory and "may" is permissive.
SITUS - Location.
SOVEREIGN - A person, body or state in which independent and supreme authority is vested.
STARE DECISIS - To follow decided cases.

STATE - "State" means this State, unless applied to the different parts of the United States. In the latter case, it includes any state, district, commonwealth, territory or insular possession of the United States, including the District of Columbia.

STATEMENT - (a) Oral or written verbal expression or (b) nonverbal conduct of a person intended by him as a substitute for oral or written verbal expression.

STATUTE - An act of the legislature. Includes a treaty.

STATUTE OF LIMITATION - A statute limiting the time to bring an action after the right of action has arisen.

STAY - To hold in abeyance an order of a court.

STIPULATION - Any agreement made by opposing attorneys regulating any matter incidental to the proceedings or trial.

SUBORDINATION (AGREEMENT) - An agreement making one's rights inferior to or of a lower rank than another's.

SUBORNATION - The crime of procuring a person to lie or to make false statements to a court.

SUBPOENA - A writ or order directed to a person, and requiring his attendance at a particular time and place to testify as a witness.

SUBPOENA DUCES TECUM - A subpoena used, not only for the purpose of compelling witnesses to attend in court, but also requiring them to bring with them books or documents which may be in their possession, and which may tend to elucidate the subject matter of the trial.

SUBROGATION - The substituting of one for another as a creditor, the new creditor succeeding to the former's rights.

SUBSIDY - A government grant to assist a private enterprise deemed advantageous to the public.

SUI GENERIS - Of the same kind.

SUIT - Any civil proceeding by a person or persons against another or others in a court of justice by which the plaintiff pursues the remedies afforded him by law.

SUMMONS - A notice to a defendant that an action against him has been commenced and requiring him to appear in court and answer the complaint.

SUPRA - Above; this word occurring by itself in a book refers the reader to a previous part of the book.

SURETY - A person who binds himself for the payment of a sum of money, or for the performance of something else, for another.

SURPLUSAGE - Extraneous or unnecessary matter.

SURVIVORSHIP - A term used when a person becomes entitled to property by reason of his having survived another person who had an interest in the property.

SUSPEND SENTENCE - Hold back a sentence pending good behavior of prisoner.

SYLLABUS - A note prefixed to a report, especially a case, giving a brief statement of the court's ruling on different issues of the case.

T

TALESMAN - Person summoned to fill a panel of jurors.

TENANT - One who holds or possesses lands by any kind of right or title; also, one who has the temporary use and occupation of real property owned by another person (landlord), the duration and terms of his tenancy being usually fixed by an instrument called "a lease."

TENDER - An offer of money; an expression of willingness to perform a contract according to its terms.

TERM - When used with reference to a court, it signifies the period of time during which the court holds a session, usually of several weeks or months duration.

TESTAMENTARY - Pertaining to a will or the administration of a will.
TESTATOR (male)
TESTATRIX (female) - One who makes or has made a testament or will.
TESTIFY (TESTIMONY) - To give evidence under oath as a witness.
TO WIT - That is to say; namely.
TORT - Wrong; injury to the person.
TRANSITORY - Passing from place to place.
TRESPASS - Entry into another's ground, illegally.
TRIAL - The examination of a cause, civil or criminal, before a judge who has jurisdiction over it, according to the laws of the land.
TRIER OF FACT - Includes (a) the jury and (b) the court when the court is trying an issue of fact other than one relating to the admissibility of evidence.
TRUST - A right of property, real or personal, held by one party for the benefit of another.
TRUSTEE - One who lawfully holds property in custody for the benefit of another.

U

UNAVAILABLE AS A WITNESS - The declarant is (1) Exempted or precluded on the ground of privilege from testifying concerning the matter to which his statement is relevant; (2) Disqualified from testifying to the matter; (3) Dead or unable to attend or to testify at the hearing because of then existing physical or mental illness or infirmity; (4) Absent from the hearing and the court is unable to compel his attendance by its process; or (5) Absent from the hearing and the proponent of his statement has exercised reasonable diligence but has been unable to procure his attendance by the court's process.
ULTRA VIRES - Acts beyond the scope and power of a corporation, association, etc.
UNILATERAL - One-sided; obligation upon, or act of one party.
USURY - Unlawful interest on a loan.

V

VACATE - To set aside; to move out.
VARIANCE - A discrepancy or disagreement between two instruments or two aspects of the same case, which by law should be consistent.
VENDEE - A purchaser or buyer.
VENDOR - The person who transfers property by sale, particularly real estate; the term "seller" is used more commonly for one who sells personal property.
VENIREMEN - Persons ordered to appear to serve on a jury or composing a panel of jurors.
VENUE - The place at which an action is tried, generally based on locality or judicial district in which an injury occurred or a material fact happened.
VERDICT - The formal decision or finding of a jury.
VERIFY - To confirm or substantiate by oath.
VEST - To accrue to.
VOID - Having no legal force or binding effect.
VOIR DIRE - Preliminary examination of a witness or a juror to test competence, interest, prejudice, etc.

W

WAIVE - To give up a right.
WAIVER - The intentional or voluntary relinquishment of a known right.
WARRANT (WARRANTY) (v.) - To promise that a certain fact or state of facts, in relation to the subject matter, is, or shall be, as it is represented to be.

WARRANT (n.) - A writ issued by a judge, or other competent authority, addressed to a sheriff, or other officer, requiring him to arrest the person therein named, and bring him before the judge or court to answer or be examined regarding the offense with which he is charged.

WRIT - An order or process issued in the name of the sovereign or in the name of a court or judicial officer, commanding the performance or nonperformance of some act.

WRITING - Handwriting, typewriting, printing, photostating, photographing and every other means of recording upon any tangible thing any form of communication or representation, including letters, words, pictures, sounds, or symbols, or combinations thereof.

WRITINGS AND RECORDINGS - Consists of letters, words, or numbers, or their equivalent, set down by handwriting, typewriting, printing, photostating, photographing, magnetic impulse, mechanical or electronic recording, or other form of data compilation.

Y

YEA AND NAY - Yes and no.

YELLOW DOG CONTRACT - A contract by which employer requires employee to sign an instrument promising as condition that he will not join a union during its continuance, and will be discharged if he does join.

Z

ZONING - The division of a city by legislative regulation into districts and the prescription and application in each district of regulations having to do with structural and architectural designs of buildings and of regulations prescribing use to which buildings within designated districts may be put.